# CHRISTMAS MOVIE TRIVIA

# 2

Publications International, Ltd.

ISBN: 978-1-64030-404-8

Manufactured in Canada.

8 7 6 5 4 3 2 1

# Table of Contents

THE MUPPET CHRISTMAS CAROL . . . . . . . . . . . . . . . . . . . . . 5

LOVE ACTUALLY . . . . . . . . . . . . . . . . . . . . . . . . . . . . . . . . . . 19

THE FAMILY STONE . . . . . . . . . . . . . . . . . . . . . . . . . . . . . 35

THE NIGHTMARE BEFORE CHRISTMAS . . . . . . . . . . . . . . . . 49

THE YEAR WITHOUT A SANTA CLAUS . . . . . . . . . . . . . . . . 65

CHRISTMAS WITH THE KRANKS . . . . . . . . . . . . . . . . . . . . 79

JINGLE ALL THE WAY . . . . . . . . . . . . . . . . . . . . . . . . . . . . 93

DR. SEUSS' HOW THE GRINCH STOLE
CHRISTMAS (LIVE ACTION) . . . . . . . . . . . . . . . . . . . . . 109

HOME ALONE . . . . . . . . . . . . . . . . . . . . . . . . . . . . . . . . . . . . .125

HOME ALONE 2: LOST IN NEW YORK . . . . . . . . . . . . . . . . . .137

GREMLINS . . . . . . . . . . . . . . . . . . . . . . . . . . . . . . . . . . . . . . 151

MIRACLE ON 34TH STREET . . . . . . . . . . . . . . . . . . . . . . . . 165

PLANES, TRAINS AND AUTOMOBILES . . . . . . . . . . . . . . . . .179

THE SHOP AROUND THE CORNER . . . . . . . . . . . . . . . . . . . 193

MIXED NUTS . . . . . . . . . . . . . . . . . . . . . . . . . . . . . . . . . . . .205

ELF . . . . . . . . . . . . . . . . . . . . . . . . . . . . . . . . . . . . . . . . . . .217

IT'S A WONDERFUL LIFE . . . . . . . . . . . . . . . . . . . . . . . . . . 235

BAD SANTA . . . . . . . . . . . . . . . . . . . . . . . . . . . . . . . . . . . .251

THE POLAR EXPRESS . . . . . . . . . . . . . . . . . . . . . . . . . . . . 263

# The Muppet Christmas Carol

**1.** When was *The Muppet Christmas Carol* released?

    **A.** 1990
    **B.** 1992
    **C.** 1994
    **D.** 1997

**2.** Who directed the movie?

    **A.** Jim Henson
    **B.** Brian Henson
    **C.** Charles Schulz
    **D.** Lee Mendelson

## ANSWERS

...............................................

1.   **B.**   1992

2.   **B.**   Brian Henson

**3.** Who wrote the classic novel, *A Christmas Carol*, that the movie was based on?

    **A.** Mark Twain
    **B.** Mary Shelley
    **C.** Charles Dickens
    **D.** Bram Stoker

**4.** In what city does the movie take place?

    **A.** London
    **B.** New York City
    **C.** Paris
    **D.** Detroit

**5.** Which Muppet is the main narrator of the story?

    **A.** Kermit the Frog
    **B.** Scooter
    **C.** Gonzo
    **D.** Rowlf the Dog

# ANSWERS

. . . . . . . . . . . . . . . . . . . . . . . . . . . . . . . . . . . . . . . .

**3.** **C.** Charles Dickens

**4.** **A.** London

**5.** **C.** Gonzo

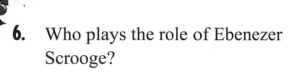

**6.** Who plays the role of Ebenezer Scrooge?

    **A.** Sean Connery
    **B.** Morgan Freeman
    **C.** George Carlin
    **D.** Michael Caine

**7.** What does Scrooge do when two men come to collect money to buy food for the poor?

    **A.** He gives them a couple dollars
    **B.** He says the poor are already looked after by prisons and workhouses
    **C.** He gives them a lot of money but is unhappy about it
    **D.** He yells at them to leave

**8.** Who warns Scrooge to repent for his greedy behavior, or else face punishment in the afterlife?

    **A.** His family
    **B.** His old girlfriend
    **C.** His late business partners
    **D.** His first grade teacher

. . . . . . . . . . . . . . . . . . . . . . . . . . . . . . . . . . . . . . . . .

**6.** **D.** Michael Caine

**7.** **B.** He says the poor are already looked after by prisons and workhouses

**8.** **C.** His late business partners

9. Who is Scrooge's nephew?

    **A.** Tim
    **B.** Fred
    **C.** Danny
    **D.** Sam

10. What does Fozziwig's factory produce?

    **A.** Tires
    **B.** Rubber chickens
    **C.** Canned goods
    **D.** Staplers

11. Why does Belle, the young woman Scrooge was in love with, leave him?

    **A.** She meets another man
    **B.** Her family is enemies with Scrooge's family
    **C.** Scrooge tells her an offensive joke
    **D.** Scrooge chooses money over her

12. Which Muppet plays the role of Tiny Tim?

    **A.** Miss Piggy
    **B.** Kermit the Frog
    **C.** Robin the Frog
    **D.** Rowlf

# ANSWERS

· · · · · · · · · · · · · · · · · · · · · · · · · · · · · · · · · · · · · · · · · · · · ·

**9.** **B.** Fred

**10.** **B.** Rubber chickens

**11.** **D.** Scrooge chooses money over her

**12.** **C.** Robin the Frog

**13.** Which of the following is NOT a ghost that interacts with Scrooge?

    **A.** The Ghost of Christmas Now
    **B.** The Ghost of Christmas Present
    **C.** The Ghost of Christmas Past
    **D.** The Ghost of Christmas Future

**14.** What eventually convinces Scrooge to change his ways?

    **A.** He loses all his money
    **B.** He learns that everyone will be happier once he is dead
    **C.** Belle, the woman he once loved, takes him back
    **D.** Tiny Tim dies

**15.** How does Scrooge celebrate his newfound zest for life on Christmas Day?

    **A.** He burns his money
    **B.** He adopts Tiny Tim as his own
    **C.** He quits his job and moves to a new city
    **D.** He throws a Christmas feast and gives gifts to characters he has wronged

. . . . . . . . . . . . . . . . . . . . . . . . . . . . . . . . . . . . . . . . . . .

**13.**    **A.**    The Ghost of Christmas Now

**14.**    **B.**    He learns that everyone will be happier once he is dead

**15.**    **D.**    He throws a Christmas feast and gives gifts to characters he has wronged

### 16. TRUE OR FALSE:

*The Muppet Christmas Carol* was the first Muppet movie to focus on a human character.

### 17. TRUE OR FALSE:

Jim Henson, the creator of the Muppets, died in 1991.

### 18. TRUE OR FALSE:

*The Muppet Christmas Carol* is the third Muppets feature film.

### 19. TRUE OR FALSE:

*The Muppet Christmas Carol* is the first Muppets movie made without Jim Henson.

# ANSWERS

......................................................

**16.** **TRUE**

**17.** **FALSE:** He died in 1990.

**18.** **FALSE:** It's the fourth.

**19.** **TRUE**

## 20. TRUE OR FALSE:

The movie was initially supposed to be a television movie, not a feature film.

## 21. TRUE OR FALSE:

The movie was filmed on the actual streets of London.

## 22. TRUE OR FALSE:

Many people consider *The Muppet Christmas Carol* one of the truest adaptations of the original story.

## 23. TRUE OR FALSE:

The Christmas Spirit characters were not pre-existing Muppet characters; they were specially-created for this movie.

## ANSWERS

· · · · · · · · · · · · · · · · · · · · · · · · · · · · · · · · · · · · · · · · ·

**20.** **TRUE**

**21.** **FALSE:** A special set had to be made to accommodate the puppeteers.

**22.** **TRUE**

**23.** **TRUE**

# Love Actually

**1.** What year did *Love Actually* come out?

    **A.** 2001

    **B.** 2002

    **C.** 2003

    **D.** 2004

**2.** What airport is mentioned in the movie's opening monologue?

    **A.** Heathrow Airport

    **B.** O'Hare Airport

    **C.** Charles De Gaulle Airport

    **D.** JFK Airport

## ANSWERS

. . . . . . . . . . . . . . . . . . . . . . . . . . . . . . . . . . . . . . . .

**1.**   **C.**   2003

**2.**   **A.**   Heathrow Airport

**3.** What big event is mentioned in the opening monologue?

    **A.** The start of the new millennium
    **B.** The U.S. invasion of Iraq
    **C.** The introduction of the iPod
    **D.** September 11, 2001

**4.** What is Billy Mack's advice to children?

    **A.** Stay in school
    **B.** Don't talk to strangers
    **C.** Don't buy drugs
    **D.** Follow your dreams

**5.** What song spontaneously plays at Juliet and Peter's wedding?

    **A.** "My Girl"
    **B.** "All You Need Is Love"
    **C.** "L-O-V-E"
    **D.** "Love Me Tender"

. . . . . . . . . . . . . . . . . . . . . . . . . . . . . . . . . . . . . . . . . . . .

**3.**   **D.**   September 11, 2001

**4.**   **C.**   Don't buy drugs

**5.**   **B.**   "All You Need Is Love"

**6.** Why is Mark so rude to Juliet?

    **A.** He's secretly in love with her
    **B.** He hates her for no reason
    **C.** Her brother killed his brother
    **D.** He thinks she's shallow

**7.** Why does Jamie decide to go on vacation in the French countryside?

    **A.** He loses his job
    **B.** He's trying to improve his French
    **C.** He's taking a class on French cooking
    **D.** He finds out his girlfriend is cheating on him

**8.** Where is Jamie's housekeeper from?

    **A.** England
    **B.** Portugal
    **C.** Spain
    **D.** France

# ANSWERS

· · · · · · · · · · · · · · · · · · · · · · · · · · · · · · · · · · · ·

**6.**    **A.**    He's secretly in love with her

**7.**    **D.**    He finds out his girlfriend is cheating on him

**8.**    **B.**    Portugal

**9.** For whom does Harry buy a necklace at the department store?

    **A.** His wife

    **B.** His secretary

    **C.** His daughter

    **D.** Himself

**10.** Who makes inappropriate advances on Natalie?

    **A.** The U.S. President

    **B.** The Prime Minister

    **C.** The German Chancellor

    **D.** The Prince of Wales

**11.** Which actor plays the role of the U.S. President?

    **A.** Matthew McConaughey

    **B.** Bruce Willis

    **C.** David Spade

    **D.** Billy Bob Thornton

# ANSWERS

· · · · · · · · · · · · · · · · · · · · · · · · · · · · · · · · · ·

**9.**    **B.**    His secretary

**10.**    **A.**    The U.S. President

**11.**    **D.**    Billy Bob Thornton

**12.** Why is Sam not upset about the passing of his mother?

    **A.** He didn't like her

    **B.** He is distracted because he is in love

    **C.** He is too stressed out about the Christmas show

    **D.** He never knew his mother

**13.** How long has Sarah been working at Harry's company?

    **A.** Two years, seven months, three days, and two hours

    **B.** Two years, three months, two days, and seven hours

    **C.** Three years, seven months, two days, and two hours

    **D.** Seven years, two months, three days, and two hours

**14.** What interrupts Sarah and Karl kissing?

    **A.** A snow storm

    **B.** A phone call from their boss

    **C.** A fire that starts in the kitchen

    **D.** A phone call from Sarah's brother

. . . . . . . . . . . . . . . . . . . . . . . . . . . . . . . . . . . . . . . . .

**12.**   **B.**   He is distracted because he is in love

**13.**   **A.**   Two years, seven months, three days, and two hours

**14.**   **D.**   A phone call from Sarah's brother

**15.** Why does Colin decide to go to America?

    **A.** For a better job

    **B.** London is getting too expensive

    **C.** American girls love English accents

    **D.** He is on the run from local law enforcement

**16.** What U.S. state does Colin buy a plane ticket to?

    **A.** Indiana

    **B.** Wisconsin

    **C.** Illinois

    **D.** Ohio

**17.** How many different stories are followed throughout *Love Actually*?

    **A.** 10

    **B.** 13

    **C.** 15

    **D.** 16

## ANSWERS

. . . . . . . . . . . . . . . . . . . . . . . . . . . . . . . . . . . . . . . . . . . . . . .

**15.**   **C.**   American girls love English accents

**16.**   **B.**   Wisconsin

**17.**   **A.**   10

**18.** What animal does Harry and Karen's daughter dress as for the Christmas show?

    **A.** A donkey
    **B.** A dove
    **C.** A lamb
    **D.** A lobster

**19.** Who is hosting the party where Billy Mack celebrates his single hitting number one on the charts?

    **A.** Sir Elton John
    **B.** Sir Paul McCartney
    **C.** Billy Joel
    **D.** Rod Stewart

**20.** What song does Joanna sing at the Christmas show?

    **A.** "White Christmas"
    **B.** "Santa Baby"
    **C.** "All I Want for Christmas Is You"
    **D.** "Last Christmas"

# ANSWERS

· · · · · · · · · · · · · · · · · · · · · · · · · · · · · · · · · ·

**18.** **D.** A lobster

**19.** **A.** Sir Elton John

**20.** **C.** "All I Want for Christmas is You"

### 21.  TRUE OR FALSE:

Sam learns how to play the guitar in order to impress Joanna.

### 22.  TRUE OR FALSE:

Jamie learns Portuguese so he can communicate with Aurelia.

### 23.  TRUE OR FALSE:

Jamie's girlfriend cheats on him with his best friend.

### 24.  TRUE OR FALSE:

Harry gives Karen a Joan Baez CD for Christmas.

### 25.  TRUE OR FALSE:

Natalie's boyfriend breaks up with her because he thinks she's fat.

· · · · · · · · · · · · · · · · · · · · · · · · · · · · · · · · · · · · · · · · · · · · · · · · · · · · · · · · · ·

**21.** **FALSE:** He learns how to play the drums.

**22.** **TRUE**

**23.** **FALSE:** She cheats on him with his brother.

**24.** **FALSE:** He gives her a Joni Mitchell CD.

**25.** **TRUE**

# The Family Stone

1. When was *The Family Stone* released?
   **A.** 2003
   **B.** 2004
   **C.** 2005
   **D.** 2006

2. Who plays the role of Meredith?
   **A.** Sarah Michelle Gellar
   **B.** Jennifer Garner
   **C.** Sarah Jessica Parker
   **D.** Kim Cattrall

## ANSWERS

...................................................

**1.** **C.** 2005

**2.** **C.** Sarah Jessica Parker

3. Which member of the Stone family is hearing impaired?

   **A.** Everett
   **B.** Sybil
   **C.** Amy
   **D.** Thad

4. Why does the Stone family dislike Meredith?

   **A.** She only talks about herself
   **B.** She's uptight and a workaholic
   **C.** She's not ambitious enough to be dating Everett
   **D.** She's only with Everett for his money

5. Why does Everett get angry with his mother?

   **A.** She will not give him her mother's wedding ring to give to Meredith
   **B.** She purposely gives Meredith peanut butter despite knowing she has a serious nut allergy
   **C.** She yells at her husband in front of the entire family
   **D.** She cancels her annual Christmas party

. . . . . . . . . . . . . . . . . . . . . . . . . . . . . . . . . . . . . . .

**3.** **D.** Thad

**4.** **B.** She's uptight and a workaholic

**5.** **A.** She will not give him her mother's wedding ring to give to Meredith

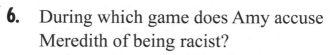

**6.** During which game does Amy accuse Meredith of being racist?

    **A.** Pictionary
    **B.** Scrabble
    **C.** Monopoly
    **D.** Charades

**7.** Who does Meredith ask to join her at the Stone family's Christmas?

    **A.** Her mother
    **B.** Her sister
    **C.** Her best friend
    **D.** Her ex-boyfriend

**8.** What happens when Julie is getting off the bus?

    **A.** The door slams in her face
    **B.** The driver yells profanities at her
    **C.** Someone pushes her
    **D.** She trips and falls

**9.** What is Everett allergic to that Meredith puts in her breakfast casserole?

    **A.** Mushrooms
    **B.** Eggplant
    **C.** Onions
    **D.** Oregano

# ANSWERS

· · · · · · · · · · · · · · · · · · · · · · · · · · · · · · · · · · · · · · · · · ·

**6.**  **D.**  Charades

**7.**  **B.**  Her sister

**8.**  **D.**  She trips and falls

**9.**  **A.**  Mushrooms

**10.** What does Meredith make an offensive comment about at dinner?

    **A.** Thad and Patrick being gay

    **B.** The family's financial situation

    **C.** The upcoming presidential election

    **D.** Patrick's race

**11.** Who does Meredith invite over for breakfast on Christmas morning?

    **A.** Her ex-boyfriend

    **B.** Everett's ex-girlfriend

    **C.** Amy's high school boyfriend

    **D.** The Stone family's estranged son

**12.** What has Sybil been diagnosed with that she keeps hidden from her children?

    **A.** Breast cancer

    **B.** Lung cancer

    **C.** Multiple sclerosis

    **D.** Diabetes

· · · · · · · · · · · · · · · · · · · · · · · · · · · · · · · · · · · · · ·

**10.** **A.** Thad and Patrick being gay

**11.** **C.** Amy's high school boyfriend

**12.** **A.** Breast cancer

**13.** Where does Meredith wake up after having gotten drunk at the bar?

    **A.** Still at the bar
    **B.** Ben's bed
    **C.** Everett's bed
    **D.** The inn where she is staying

**14.** What does Meredith give each of the Stone family members as a Christmas present?

    **A.** A cheesy souvenir from New York City
    **B.** A copy of their favorite Christmas movie
    **C.** A framed picture of their childhood home that burned down in a mysterious fire
    **D.** A framed picture of their mother when she was pregnant

**15.** What happens when Amy and Sybil go into the kitchen to apologize to Meredith?

    **A.** They hit Meredith with the door
    **B.** Meredith drops her breakfast casserole
    **C.** Amy slips and falls
    **D.** All of the above

## ANSWERS

· · · · · · · · · · · · · · · · · · · · · · · · · · · · · · · · ·

**13.**   **B.**   Ben's bed

**14.**   **D.**   A framed picture of their
mother when she was pregnant

**15.**   **D.**   All of the above

**16.   TRUE OR FALSE:**

Everyone in the Stone family knows
sign language.


**17.   TRUE OR FALSE:**

Everett is in love with Julie from the
first moment he sees her.


**18.   TRUE OR FALSE:**

Thad and Patrick are unable to adopt a
baby at the end of the movie.


**19.   TRUE OR FALSE:**

When the movie flashes forward to
next year, Sybil has died.

# ANSWERS

. . . . . . . . . . . . . . . . . . . . . . . . . . . . . . . . . . . . . . . . .

**16.** **TRUE**

**17.** **TRUE**

**18.** **FALSE:** They are ultimately able to adopt.

**19.** **TRUE**

### 20. TRUE OR FALSE:

Meredith and Everett end up getting married.

### 21. TRUE OR FALSE:

Rachel McAdams was nominated for a Teen Choice Award for her portrayal of Amy.

### 22. TRUE OR FALSE:

The Stone family likes Meredith more than they like Julie.

### 23. TRUE OR FALSE:

Everett walks in on Meredith sleeping in his brother's bed.

### 24. TRUE OR FALSE:

When Everett asks Julie to try on his grandmother's old ring, it fits her perfectly.

# ANSWERS

. . . . . . . . . . . . . . . . . . . . . . . . . . . . . . . . . . .

**20.** **FALSE:** Meredith marries Ben and Everett marries Julie.

**21.** **TRUE**

**22.** **FALSE:** The family loves Julie when they first meet her and they hate Meredith.

**23.** **FALSE:** Kelly walks in on Meredith sleeping in Ben's bed.

**24.** **FALSE:** It gets stuck on her finger.

# The Nightmare Before Christmas

1. What year was *The Nightmare Before Christmas* released?

   **A.** 1993
   **B.** 1994
   **C.** 1995
   **D.** 1997

2. What is the name of the town where Jack Skellington lives?

   **A.** Christmas Town
   **B.** New York City
   **C.** Pumpkin Town
   **D.** Halloween Town

## ANSWERS

· · · · · · · · · · · · · · · · · · · · · · · · · · · · · · · · · · · · · · ·

**1.**   **A.**   1993

**2.**   **D.**   Halloween Town

**3.** Who produced and created the movie?

    **A.** Johnny Depp

    **B.** Steven Spielberg

    **C.** Tim Burton

    **D.** Danny Elfman

**4.** In what style of animation is the movie made?

    **A.** Hand-drawn/traditional animation

    **B.** 3D computer animation

    **C.** Vector-based animation

    **D.** Stop motion animation

**5.** What is Jack's official title?

    **A.** The Pumpkin King

    **B.** President

    **C.** Minister of Horror

    **D.** Chief Pumpkin Officer

## ANSWERS

. . . . . . . . . . . . . . . . . . . . . . . . . . . . . . . . . . . . . . .

**3.**    **C.**    Tim Burton

**4.**    **D.**    Stop motion animation

**5.**    **A.**    The Pumpkin King

**6.** What is the name of Jack's dog?

    **A.** Scraps

    **B.** Boo

    **C.** Zero

    **D.** Bones

**7.** How does Sally poison Dr. Finklestein?

    **A.** She slips nightshade into his soup

    **B.** She sprinkles rat poison over him while he is sleeping

    **C.** She replaces his daily vitamins with cyanide

    **D.** She mixes radioactive waste in with his orange juice

**8.** How does Jack first encounter Christmas Town?

    **A.** He sees it in a movie he is watching about "fictional holidays"

    **B.** He is kidnapped by Santa Claus himself

    **C.** He reads about it in a book he finds in his grandfather's attic

    **D.** He stumbles upon the portal to it while walking through the woods

# ANSWERS

. . . . . . . . . . . . . . . . . . . . . . . . . . . . . . . . . . . . .

**6.**  **C.**  Zero

**7.**  **A.**  She slips nightshade into his soup

**8.**  **D.**  He stumbles upon the portal to it while walking through the woods

**9.** What does Jack think Santa Claus's name is?

    **A.** Sad Dog Paws

    **B.** Sammy Jaws

    **C.** Scary Gauze

    **D.** Sandy Claws

**10.** Which is NOT a task that Jack gives to the residents of his town in his plan to take over Christmas Town?

    **A.** Kidnap Santa Claus

    **B.** Make Jack a Santa suit

    **C.** Put worms in gingerbread cookies

    **D.** Make scary reindeer

**11.** Who do the trick-or-treaters kidnap after mistaking them for Santa?

    **A.** The Easter Bunny

    **B.** The Tooth Fairy

    **C.** The New Years Baby

    **D.** Cupid

· · · · · · · · · · · · · · · · · · · · · · · · · · · · · · · · · ·

**9.** **D.** Sandy Claws

**10.** **C.** Put worms in gingerbread cookies

**11.** **A.** The Easter Bunny

**12.** What is Oogie Boogie addicted to?

    **A.** Drugs
    **B.** Gambling
    **C.** Candy
    **D.** The Home Shopping Network

**13.** What happens when Jack delivers the Halloween-themed Christmas presents to Christmas Town?

    **A.** Everyone celebrates together in the spirit of Christmas
    **B.** One of the presents, a tiny monster, eats the hand of a small child
    **C.** The citizens of Christmas Town demand more Halloween presents
    **D.** Everyone is scared and screams

**14.** How do the residents of Christmas Town get rid of Jack?

    **A.** They sign a petition asking him to leave
    **B.** They call the military, who proceed to blast him out of the sky
    **C.** They shoot slingshots at him
    **D.** They board up their chimneys so he can't get into their homes

. . . . . . . . . . . . . . . . . . . . . . . . . . . . . . . . . . . . . .

**12.**  **B.**  Gambling

**13.**  **D.**  Everyone is scared and screams

**14.**  **B.**  They call the military, who proceed to blast him out of the sky

**15.** What happens when Sally attempts to free Santa?

    **A.** She successfully rescues him

    **B.** She gets captured by Oogie Boogie

    **C.** She is knocked unconscious by one of Oogie's henchmen

    **D.** She slips and falls into a vat of lava

**16.** When Jack pulls a thread to unravel Oogie, what spills out of him?

    **A.** Bugs

    **B.** Cotton stuffing

    **C.** Halloween candy

    **D.** Mysterious slime

**17.** What does Santa do to Halloween Town to show he forgives Jack?

    **A.** He gives everyone presents

    **B.** He teaches them the true meaning of Christmas

    **C.** He makes it snow

    **D.** He makes Christmas trees grow all around town

# ANSWERS

· · · · · · · · · · · · · · · · · · · · · · · · · · · · · · · · · · · ·

**15.**    **B.**    She gets captured by Oogie Boogie

**16.**    **A.**    Bugs

**17.**    **C.**    He makes it snow

## 18. TRUE OR FALSE:

Chris Sarandon voiced Jack's speaking and singing voice.

## 19. TRUE OR FALSE:

*The Nightmare Before Christmas* was originally developed as a short film.

## 20. TRUE OR FALSE:

*The Nightmare Before Christmas* was nominated for an Academy Award.

## 21. TRUE OR FALSE:

The movie initially started out as a short story.

## ANSWERS

. . . . . . . . . . . . . . . . . . . . . . . . . . . . . . . . . . . . . . . . .

**18.**    **FALSE:**    Chris Sarandon voiced Jack's speaking voice, but Danny Elfman provided his singing voice.

**19.**    **TRUE**

**20.**    **TRUE**

**21.**    **FALSE:**    It initially started out as a poem.

## 22. TRUE OR FALSE:

Jack and Sally end up confessing their love for one another at the end of the movie.

## 23. TRUE OR FALSE:

When Jack is shot down by the military, he gives up all hope for any holiday.

## 24. TRUE OR FALSE:

Tim Burton directed *The Nightmare Before Christmas*.

## 25. TRUE OR FALSE:

The townspeople hate the snow that Santa makes.

## 26. TRUE OR FALSE:

The movie was initially supposed to be a television movie, not a feature film.

## ANSWERS

. . . . . . . . . . . . . . . . . . . . . . . . . . . . . . . . . . . . . . . . . . .

**22.** **TRUE**

**23.** **FALSE:** By seeing what a disaster Christmas is, Jack's love for Halloween is revived.

**24.** **FALSE:** It was directed by Henry Selick because Burton was busy directing *Batman Returns*.

**25.** **FALSE:** They are confused at first, but eventually have fun in the snow.

**26.** **TRUE**

# The Year Without a Santa Claus

1.  What year was *The Year Without a Santa Claus* released?

    **A.** 1970
    **B.** 1972
    **C.** 1973
    **D.** 1974

2.  On what station was the movie originally broadcast?

    **A.** NBC
    **B.** ABC
    **C.** CBS
    **D.** FOX

# ANSWERS

· · · · · · · · · · · · · · · · · · · · · · · · · · · · · · · · · · · · · · · · · · ·

**1.** **D.** 1974

**2.** **B.** ABC

**3.** Who voices Santa Claus?

    **A.** Fred Astaire

    **B.** Mickey Rooney

    **C.** Gene Kelly

    **D.** Clark Gable

**4.** Who narrates the story?

    **A.** Santa

    **B.** Santa's elves

    **C.** Mrs. Claus

    **D.** Mother Nature

**5.** Why does Santa announce that Christmas is cancelled?

    **A.** He is feeling under the weather

    **B.** His doctor tells him no one cares about Christmas

    **C.** He converts to Judaism

    **D.** Both A and B

**6.** What is the name of the town where the elves land?

    **A.** Anytown, USA

    **B.** Pleasanttown, USA

    **C.** Southtown, USA

    **D.** Smalltown, USA

## ANSWERS

. . . . . . . . . . . . . . . . . . . . . . . . . . . . . . . . . . . . . . .

**3.** **B.** Mickey Rooney

**4.** **C.** Mrs. Claus

**5.** **D.** Both A and B

**6.** **C.** Southtown, USA

**7.** Which reindeer do Jingle and Jangle bring with them on their journey to find someone who still cares about Santa?

**A.** Dasher
**B.** Prancer
**C.** Donner
**D.** Vixen

**8.** When Vixen gets captured by the dog catcher, the mayor says to Jingle and Jangle that he will release her on what condition?

**A.** If they pay him a ransom
**B.** If they make it snow on Christmas Day
**C.** If they promise to give the kids in the town the best Christmas presents
**D.** If they let him take another reindeer from the North Pole to keep as a pet

**9.** Which reindeer does Santa take when he goes to rescue the elves?

**A.** Comet
**B.** Dancer
**C.** Dasher
**D.** Vixen

## ANSWERS

..............................................

**7.** **D.** Vixen

**8.** **B.** If they make it snow on Christmas Day

**9.** **C.** Dasher

**10.** Why does Vixen fall ill?

    **A.** She eats some bad fish

    **B.** She runs out of Christmas spirit

    **C.** She is allergic to the grass in Southtown

    **D.** She is not accustomed to the warm weather

**11.** Why do the kids in town not believe in Santa?

    **A.** They never get what they ask for on Christmas

    **B.** Santa is for little kids

    **C.** Their parents told them Santa isn't real

    **D.** One of them has visited the North Pole and didn't see Santa there

**12.** What are the names of the Miser brothers, whom the elves visit?

    **A.** Snow Miser and Heat Miser

    **B.** Cold Miser and Hot Miser

    **C.** Winter Miser and Summer Miser

    **D.** Ice Miser and Sun Miser

# ANSWERS

**10.**    **D.**    She is not accustomed to the warm weather

**11.**    **B.**    Santa is for little kids

**12.**    **A.**    Snow Miser and Heat Miser

**13.** How does Mrs. Claus eventually get the Miser brothers to compromise and let it snow in Southtown?

- **A.** She pays them a lot of money
- **B.** She threatens them with coal in their stockings on Christmas
- **C.** She cries and they feel bad for her
- **D.** She talks to their mother

**14.** What song does a little girl sing to Santa when she finds out he cancelled Christmas?

- **A.** "I'll Be Home for Christmas"
- **B.** "Please Come Home for Christmas"
- **C.** "Have Yourself a Merry Little Christmas"
- **D.** "Blue Christmas"

**15.** What name does the mayor give to a street in Southtown after it snows?

- **A.** Santa Claus Lane
- **B.** Candy Cane Lane
- **C.** Snow Street
- **D.** Arctic Avenue

· · · · · · · · · · · · · · · · · · · · · · · · · · · · · · · · · · · · · · ·

**13.**    **D.**    She talks to their mother

**14.**    **D.**    "Blue Christmas"

**15.**    **A.**    Santa Claus Lane

## 16. TRUE OR FALSE:

*The Year Without a Santa Claus* was originally a book.

## 17. TRUE OR FALSE:

The role of Mrs. Claus was Shirley Booth's final acting credit.

## 18. TRUE OR FALSE:

Santa Claus wakes up with a cold on Christmas Day.

## 19. TRUE OR FALSE:

Iggy Thistlewhite's parents say that they do not believe in Santa Claus.

## 20. TRUE OR FALSE:

Once they arrive in Southtown, Jingle and Jangle get a ticket for jaywalking.

## ANSWERS

· · · · · · · · · · · · · · · · · · · · · · · · · · · · · · · ·

**16.** **TRUE**

**17.** **TRUE**

**18.** **FALSE:** He gets his cold shortly after Thanksgiving.

**19.** **FALSE:** They do believe in Santa Claus.

**20.** **FALSE:** They get a ticket for "riding a vixen the wrong way down a one-way street, crossing the white line, and wearing funny-lookin' clothes on a Sunday."

## 21. TRUE OR FALSE:

Santa announces his plan to take the year off with a press release.

## 22. TRUE OR FALSE:

Iggy gets a bicycle for Christmas.

## 23. TRUE OR FALSE:

The only letter Santa receives is from the girl who sings to him, but that is enough to sway him into rethinking his plan to cancel the holiday.

## 24. TRUE OR FALSE:

Mother Nature is very angry and mean to Mrs. Claus.

## ANSWERS

· · · · · · · · · · · · · · · · · · · · · · · · · · · · · · · · · · · · · ·

**21.**     **TRUE**

**22.**     **TRUE**

**23.**     **FALSE:** Children from all over the world send him letters.

**24.**     **FALSE:** Mother Nature is very kind and wants to help Mrs. Claus.

# Christmas with the Kranks

**1.** What year was *Christmas with the Kranks* released?

    **A.** 2004
    **B.** 2005
    **C.** 2006
    **D.** 2007

**2.** In which suburb of Chicago do the Kranks live?

    **A.** Hyland Park
    **B.** Riverside
    **C.** Downers Grove
    **D.** Skokie

# ANSWERS

· · · · · · · · · · · · · · · · · · · · · · · · · · · · · · · · · · · · · · · · · · · · · · ·

1.   **A.**   2004

2.   **B.**   Riverside

3. Who plays the role of Nora Krank?

    **A.** Diane Keaton

    **B.** Jamie Lee Curtis

    **C.** Sigourney Weaver

    **D.** Molly Ringwald

4. Which director of movies such as *Home Alone, Gremlins,* and *The Goonies,* wrote and produced *Christmas with the Kranks?*

    **A.** John Hughes

    **B.** Steven Spielberg

    **C.** Chris Columbus

    **D.** Wes Anderson

5. Where does Blair, Luther and Nora Krank's daughter, go to serve as a Peace Corps volunteer?

    **A.** Rwanda

    **B.** Benin

    **C.** Argentina

    **D.** Peru

## ANSWERS

· · · · · · · · · · · · · · · · · · · · · · · · · · · · · · · · · · · · · · · · · ·

**3.** **B.** Jamie Lee Curtis

**4.** **C.** Chris Columbus

**5.** **D.** Peru

**6.** About how much money did the Kranks spend on Christmas last year?

    **A.** $4,000
    **B.** $5,000
    **C.** $6,000
    **D.** $7,000

**7.** What do the Kranks decide to do with the money they would otherwise spend on Christmas?

    **A.** Visit Blair in Peru
    **B.** Go on a Caribbean cruise
    **C.** Give it all to charity
    **D.** Remodel their home

**8.** What food does Nora try to buy at the store because it is Blair's favorite?

    **A.** Stuffing
    **B.** Honey glazed ham
    **C.** Cranberry sauce
    **D.** Turkey

## ANSWERS

· · · · · · · · · · · · · · · · · · · · · · · · · · · · · · · · · · · · · · · ·

**6.**   **C.**   $6,000

**7.**   **B.**   Go on a Caribbean cruise

**8.**   **B.**   Honey glazed ham

**9.** Why are the local police officers angry with the Kranks for cancelling Christmas?

    **A.** The Kranks always buy a calendar from them around Christmas

    **B.** The police look forward to shutting down the Kranks' Christmas party every year

    **C.** The Kranks always give the police a generous and thoughtful gift on Christmas Day

    **D.** The police are worried that not celebrating Christmas is the first step into the Kranks becoming criminals

**10.** How does Luther deter the Christmas carolers?

    **A.** He threatens them with legal action

    **B.** He glues his front door shut

    **C.** He freezes his lawn

    **D.** He builds a makeshift wall around his house using old Christmas decorations

## ANSWERS

. . . . . . . . . . . . . . . . . . . . . . . . . . . . . . . . . . . . . . .

**9.** **A.** The Kranks always buy a calendar from them around Christmas

**10.** **C.** He freezes his lawn

11. Why are the Boy Scouts angry with the Kranks for cancelling Christmas?

**A.** The Kranks always give them a ride to the annual Christmas show

**B.** The Kranks give the Boy Scouts eggnog and cookies on Christmas

**C.** The Kranks usually purchase a Christmas tree from the Boy Scouts to help with their fundraising

**D.** The Kranks let the Boy Scouts sing Christmas carols at their front door when no one else on the block wants to hear them sing

12. Why do the neighbors call the police on Luther Krank?

**A.** They think he stole a car

**B.** They think he stole his neighbor's Christmas tree

**C.** They think they see him hit a cat and drive away

**D.** They think his party is too loud

# ANSWERS

. . . . . . . . . . . . . . . . . . . . . . . . . . . . . . . . . . . . . . .

**11.**    **C.**    The Kranks usually purchase a Christmas tree from the Boy Scouts to help with their fundraising

**12.**    **B.**    They think he stole his neighbor's Christmas tree

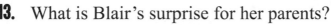

**13.** What is Blair's surprise for her parents?

    **A.** That she will come home for Christmas

    **B.** That she has a Peruvian fiancé

    **C.** She's pregnant

    **D.** Both A and B

**14.** When do the neighbors finally stop sabotaging the Kranks?

    **A.** When they see Nora Krank cry

    **B.** When Luther stubs his toe and they feel bad

    **C.** When they learn Blair is coming home

    **D.** When a mysterious stranger warns them that being mean to other people is not part of having Christmas spirit

**15.** What does Luther Krank do with his cruise tickets?

    **A.** He burns them in the Christmas fire

    **B.** He gives them to Blair and her fiancé for their honeymoon

    **C.** He gives them to Walt Scheel and his wife

    **D.** The Boy Scouts steal them from him

# ANSWERS

· · · · · · · · · · · · · · · · · · · · · · · · · · · · · · · · · ·

**13.** **D.** Both A and B

**14.** **C.** When they learn Blair is coming home

**15.** **C.** He gives them to Walt Scheel and his wife

**16. TRUE OR FALSE:**

*Christmas with the Kranks* is based on a novel by James Patterson.

**17. TRUE OR FALSE:**

*Christmas with the Kranks* got very positive reviews.

**18. TRUE OR FALSE:**

The Kranks' neighbors are worried that they will lose the contest for best-decorated street because of the Kranks not partaking in Christmas.

**19. TRUE OR FALSE:**

When Nora can't find honey glazed ham at the store she buys tuna instead.

**20. TRUE OR FALSE:**

*Christmas with the Kranks* was Tom Poston's final film.

**21. TRUE OR FALSE:**

The movie was filmed in the Chicago area.

**22. TRUE OR FALSE:**

Blair flies home with a connecting flight through the Atlanta airport.

# ANSWERS

· · · · · · · · · · · · · · · · · · · · · · · · · · · · · · · · · · · · · ·

**16.**  **FALSE:**  It is based on a novel by John Grisham.

**17.**  **FALSE:**  The film has a rating of 5% on the website Rotten Tomatoes.

**18.**  **TRUE**

**19.**  **FALSE:**  She buys smoked trout.

**20.**  **TRUE**

**21.**  **FALSE:**  It was filmed in California.

**22.**  **FALSE:**  She flies through Miami.

# Jingle All the Way

1. When was *Jingle All the Way* released?

    A. 1994
    B. 1996
    C. 1998
    D. 1999

2. Who plays the starring role of Howard Langston?

    A. Sylvester Stallone
    B. Bruce Willis
    C. Arnold Schwarzenegger
    D. Jean-Claude Van Damme

# ANSWERS

- - - - - - - - - - - - - - - - - - - - - - - - - - - - - - - - - - - - - -

**1.**   **B.**   1996

**2.**   **C.**   Arnold Schwarzenegger

**3.** What is the name of the action figure that Howard is trying to get his son for Christmas?

    **A.** Turbo Man
    **B.** Action Man
    **C.** Super-Sonic Steven
    **D.** Flashy Fred

**4.** What is Howard's profession?

    **A.** Used car salesman
    **B.** Mattress salesman
    **C.** Corporate executive
    **D.** Accountant

**5.** Why does Howard feel like he's a bad father to Jamie?

    **A.** He forgets to pick up Jamie from school
    **B.** He forgets about Jamie's karate class graduation
    **C.** He forgets about Jamie's eighth grade graduation
    **D.** He accidentally eats a cake that was meant for Jamie's birthday

**3.**    **A.**    Turbo Man

**4.**    **B.**    Mattress salesman

**5.**    **B.**    He forgets about Jamie's karate class graduation

**6.** Who plays the role of Myron Larabee, the postal worker who becomes Howard's nemesis?

    **A.** Sting
    **B.** Coolio
    **C.** Eminem
    **D.** Sinbad

**7.** Where does *Jingle All the Way* take place?

    **A.** Chicago
    **B.** New York
    **C.** Milwaukee
    **D.** The Twin Cities

**8.** Who is the secret leader of a gang of counterfeit toy makers?

    **A.** The mall Santa
    **B.** The real Santa
    **C.** Myron
    **D.** Howard's wife

# ANSWERS

. . . . . . . . . . . . . . . . . . . . . . . . . . . . . . . . . . . . . . .

**6.** **D.** Sinbad

**7.** **D.** The Twin Cities

**8.** **A.** The mall Santa

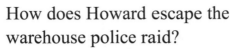

**9.** How does Howard escape the warehouse police raid?

   **A.** He hides behind an old arcade game

   **B.** He uses a toy badge to pose as a detective

   **C.** He crawls out a small window in which he almost gets stuck

   **D.** He jumps into a foam pit so the police can't see him

**10.** Howard hears a radio advertisement about a competition in which the winner will receive a free Turbo Man doll. What is the competition for?

   **A.** Singing

   **B.** Dancing

   **C.** Interior design

   **D.** Trivia

**11.** What does Myron do when he and Howard get to the radio studio?

   **A.** Threatens to blow it up

   **B.** Steals the Turbo Man doll

   **C.** Pretends to be a DJ so he can play his favorite song

   **D.** Breaks a piece of expensive equipment

# ANSWERS

9. **B.** He uses a toy badge to pose as a detective

10. **D.** Trivia

11. **A.** Threatens to blow it up

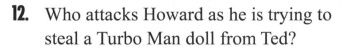

**12.** Who attacks Howard as he is trying to steal a Turbo Man doll from Ted?

- **A.** Ted
- **B.** Santa Claus
- **C.** Ted's pet reindeer
- **D.** Ted's pet dog

**13.** What happens between Ted and Liz at the parade?

- **A.** Ted gives Liz an extra Turbo Man doll to give to Jamie
- **B.** Ted hits on Liz
- **C.** Ted trash talks Howard and Liz realizes he's right
- **D.** Liz almost gets hit by a parade float and Ted rescues her

**14.** Who is Howard mistaken for when he runs into a building to hide?

- **A.** The actor posing as Turbo Man in the parade
- **B.** The mayor of the city
- **C.** Ted
- **D.** The mall Santa

# ANSWERS

· · · · · · · · · · · · · · · · · · · · · · · · · · · · · · · · · · · ·

**12.** **C.** Ted's pet reindeer

**13.** **B.** Ted hits on Liz

**14.** **A.** The actor posing as Turbo Man in the parade

**15.** What is the name of Turbo Man's arch enemy?

   **A.** EvilTron

   **B.** Hodor

   **C.** Dr. Pain

   **D.** Dementor

**16.** Why does Jamie end up giving the Turbo Man doll to Myron's son?

   **A.** He decides he's "too old for superheroes"

   **B.** He sees the pain it has caused his family and feels guilty

   **C.** He realizes that he has the "real Turbo Man at home" because of his father

   **D.** A new, cooler toy just got released and Jamie wants that instcad

**17.** What does Howard get Liz for Chrismtas?

   **A.** Nothing

   **B.** Jewelry

   **C.** The toy she wanted when she was younger that her dad never got for her

   **D.** A picture of him dressed as Turbo Man

· · · · · · · · · · · · · · · · · · · · · · · · · · · · · · · · · · · · ·

**15.** **D.** Dementor

**16.** **C.** He realizes that he has the "real Turbo Man at home" because of his father

**17.** **A.** Nothing

## 18. TRUE OR FALSE:

Arnold Schwarzenegger improvised much of his dialogue with Sinbad for the film.

## 19. TRUE OR FALSE:

Although the film was set in the Twin Cities, it was filmed mainly in Chicago.

## 20. TRUE OR FALSE:

*Jingle All the Way* was inspired by real-life competition to buy popular toys at Christmas.

## 21. TRUE OR FALSE:

*Jingle All the Way* was the third movie Schwarzenegger and Sinbad starred in together.

## 22. TRUE OR FALSE:

Turbo Man is a completely fictional toy.

# ANSWERS

. . . . . . . . . . . . . . . . . . . . . . . . . . . . . . . . . . . . .

**18.**     **TRUE**

**19.**     **FALSE:** It was filmed mainly in Minnesota.

**20.**     **TRUE**

**21.**     **FALSE:** It was their only movie together.

**22.**     **FALSE:** Turbo Man dolls are available for purchase on EBay.

### 23. TRUE OR FALSE:

When Ted hits on Liz, she hits him with a thermos of coffee.

### 24. TRUE OR FALSE:

Officer Hummel is so impressed with Howard's actions while dressed as Turbo Man that he asks him to join the police force.

### 25. TRUE OR FALSE:

Arnold Schwarzenegger punches a real reindeer in the movie.

### 26. TRUE OR FALSE:

*Jingle All the Way* is commonly considered one of the best Christmas movies of all time.

## ANSWERS

. . . . . . . . . . . . . . . . . . . . . . . . . . . . . . . . . . . . . . . . . . .

**23.** **FALSE:** She hits him with a thermos of eggnog.

**24.** **TRUE**

**25.** **FALSE:** In the scene where Howard punches the reindeer, a puppet is used.

**26.** **FALSE:** It is often included in lists of the worst Christmas movies of all time.

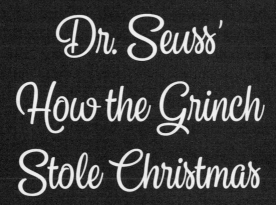

*Dr. Seuss'*
*How the Grinch Stole Christmas*
(Live Action)

**1.** Who stars as the lead role of the Grinch?

    **A.** Adam Sandler
    **B.** Jim Carrey
    **C.** Neil Patrick Harris
    **D.** Ben Stiller

**2.** How many weeks did the film spend at #1 in the United States?

    **A.** Four
    **B.** Five
    **C.** Six
    **D.** Seven

# ANSWERS

· · · · · · · · · · · · · · · · · · · · · · · · · · · · · · · · · · · · · · · · · ·

**1.**　**B.**　Jim Carrey

**2.**　**A.**　Four

**3.** The original TV special, *How the Grinch Stole Christmas,* came out in 1966. When did the live action film come out?

    **A.** 1999
    **B.** 2000
    **C.** 2001
    **D.** 2002

**4.** Where is Whoville located?

    **A.** On a marshmallow floating in a mug of hot chocolate
    **B.** On the tip of a pine needle
    **C.** On a tiny snowflake
    **D.** In an undisclosed location in the Arctic Circle

**5.** How old is Cindy Lou Who?

    **A.** Five
    **B.** Six
    **C.** Seven
    **D.** Eight

# ANSWERS

..........................................

**3.** **B.** 2000

**4.** **C.** On a tiny snowflake

**5.** **B.** Six

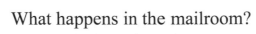

**6.** What happens in the mailroom?

**A.** The Grinch steals everyone's Christmas cards

**B.** Cindy Lou falls into the mail sorting machine and the Grinch saves her

**C.** Cindy Lou's dad almost gets hit by the mail truck

**D.** The Grinch puts smelly garlic in everyone's letters

**7.** What is the connection between the Grinch and Augustus May, the mayor of Whoville?

**A.** They were childhood best friends

**B.** They are brothers

**C.** The Grinch bullied Augustus in school

**D.** Augustus bullied the Grinch in school

**8.** What does Augustus May give the Grinch as a Christmas present?

**A.** A kit on how to be less green

**B.** A new puppy

**C.** A book about the history of Whoville

**D.** An electric shaver

. . . . . . . . . . . . . . . . . . . . . . . . . . . . . . . . . . . . . . . .

**6.**   **B.**   Cindy Lou falls into the mail sorting machine and the Grinch saves her

**7.**   **D.**   Augustus bullied the Grinch in school

**8.**   **D.**   An electric shaver

**9.** When the Grinch was a schoolboy, what caused him to lose his temper and run away to live on Mount Crumpit?

    **A.** He failed his favorite class

    **B.** He learned that he was adopted

    **C.** His classmates made fun of him for having facial hair

    **D.** He learned that Santa isn't real

**10.** How does the Grinch try to ruin the Whos' party?

    **A.** He spikes the eggnog

    **B.** He burns their Christmas tree

    **C.** He puts a spell on them to make them lose their voices and not be able to sing

    **D.** He eats all of their Christmas cookies

**11.** What does the Grinch plan to do when he realizes he did not succeed in ruining the Whos' party?

    **A.** He will steal all their presents

    **B.** He will melt all their snow

    **C.** He will turn off the power so they can't light their lights

    **D.** He will replace their Christmas cookie sprinkles with ants

# ANSWERS

. . . . . . . . . . . . . . . . . . . . . . . . . . . . . . . . . . . . . . . .

**9.**  **C.**  His classmates made fun of him for having facial hair

**10.**  **B.**  He burns their Christmas tree

**11.**  **A.**  He will steal all their presents

**12.** Who reminds the Whos that the true meaning of Christmas is to spend it with loved ones?

    **A.** The Grinch

    **B.** Cindy Lou Who

    **C.** Cindy Lou Who's dad, Lou Lou Who

    **D.** The Grinch's dog, Max

**13.** What happens to the Whos' presents?

    **A.** The Grinch burns them

    **B.** The Grinch tries to push them off a mountain

    **C.** The Grinch returns them to the store for store credit

    **D.** The Whos give them all to the Grinch in hopes that he learns the true meaning of Christmas from the gesture

**14.** What happens that makes the Grinch have a change of heart?

    **A.** His dog dies

    **B.** The Whos cast a spell on him

    **C.** He hears the Whos crying

    **D.** He hears the Whos singing

## ANSWERS

. . . . . . . . . . . . . . . . . . . . . . . . . . . . . . . . . . . . . . .

**12.**    **C.**    Cindy Lou Who's dad, Lou Lou Who

**13.**    **B.**    The Grinch tries to push them off a mountain

**14.**    **D.**    He hears the Whos singing

**15.** Who does Mayor Augustus May blame for the Grinch's evil plan?

    **A.** Himself

    **B.** Cindy Lou Who

    **C.** The Grinch

    **D.** Santa

**16.** Who almost falls off the cliff?

    **A.** Cindy Lou Who

    **B.** Max

    **C.** Mayor Augustus May

    **D.** The entire town of Whoville

**17.** How many sizes does the Grinch's heart grow?

    **A.** Two

    **B.** Three

    **C.** Four

    **D.** Five

**18.** What does Martha say when Mayor Augustus May proposes to her?

    **A.** Yes, but only if he buys her a bigger engagement ring

    **B.** No, she would like to be single for a while

    **C.** No, she would rather be with the Grinch

    **D.** Yes, but only if he starts being nicer to the Grinch

# ANSWERS

· · · · · · · · · · · · · · · · · · · · · · · · · · · · · · · · · · · · · · · · · · · · · ·

**15.** **B.** Cindy Lou Who

**16.** **A.** Cindy Lou Who

**17.** **B.** Three

**18.** **C.** No, she would rather be with the Grinch

### 19. TRUE OR FALSE:

*The Grinch* was the first Dr. Seuss book to be adapted into a full-length feature film.

### 20. TRUE OR FALSE:

Although *The Grinch* was incredibly commercially successful, it was never nominated for any awards.

### 21. TRUE OR FALSE:

The Grinch was cruel and sadistic from the moment he was born.

### 22. TRUE OR FALSE:

This film closely follows the plot of the 1966 cartoon film of the same name.

## ANSWERS

19. **TRUE**

20. **FALSE:** It was nominated for three Academy Awards, and it won the Academy Award for Best Makeup.

21. **FALSE:** The Grinch was a timid child who was driven to cruelty by bullying from his classmates.

22. **FALSE:** Since *The Grinch* was a feature length film, not a TV special, many additions were made to the story to add to its length.

### 23. TRUE OR FALSE:

The Grinch was adopted by two women when he was a baby.

### 24. TRUE OR FALSE:

At the time of its release, *The Grinch,* was the highest-grossing holiday film of all time.

### 25. TRUE OR FALSE:

When Augustus proposes to Martha, he promises her the biggest diamond in all of Whoville.

### 26. TRUE OR FALSE:

Despite winning an Academy Award, *The Grinch* was also nominated for the Golden Raspberry Awards for Worst Remake or Sequel and Worst Screenplay.

**23.** **TRUE**

**24.** **FALSE:** It was the second highest-grossing holiday film of all time after *Home Alone.*

**25.** **FALSE:** He promises her a car.

**26.** **TRUE**

# Home Alone

**1.** What year was *Home Alone* released?

   **A.** 1988
   **B.** 1990
   **C.** 1992
   **D.** 1993

**2.** What famous director wrote and produced *Home Alone?*

   **A.** Chris Columbus
   **B.** Tim Burton
   **C.** John Hughes
   **D.** Steven Spielberg

**3.** What type of pet does Buzz have that escapes in the house?

   **A.** A lizard
   **B.** A chameleon
   **C.** A tortoise
   **D.** A tarantula

# ANSWERS

························································

**1.** **B.** 1990

**2.** **C.** John Hughes

**3.** **D.** A tarantula

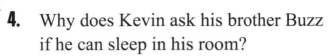

4. Why does Kevin ask his brother Buzz if he can sleep in his room?

   **A.** He knows his cousin Fuller will wet the bed

   **B.** He heard that Fuller snores loudly

   **C.** He wants to spend more quality time with Buzz

   **D.** He thinks Buzz has a more comfortable bed

5. What does Buzz tell Kevin their creepy next-door neighbor, Old Man Marley, does with the remains of the people he killed?

   **A.** Eats them

   **B.** Turns them into life-like dolls

   **C.** Sells them on the Black Market

   **D.** Uses them to salt the sidewalk

6. Later in the film, what does Kevin urge Old Man Marley to do?

   **A.** Stop murdering his neighbors

   **B.** Help him trick the burglars

   **C.** Make amends with his estranged son

   **D.** Sell his house and move somewhere warmer

# ANSWERS

· · · · · · · · · · · · · · · · · · · · · · · · · · · · · · · · · · · ·

**4.**    **A.**    He knows his cousin Fuller will wet the bed

**5.**    **D.**    Uses them to salt the sidewalk

**6.**    **C.**    Make amends with his estranged son

**7.** What does Kevin wish for after he is sent to his bedroom as punishment for fighting with Buzz?

**A.** For four cheese pizzas
**B.** For his family to disappear
**C.** For just Buzz to disappear
**D.** For a nicer family

**8.** What beverage does Fuller menacingly drink while staring at Kevin?

**A.** Coca-Cola
**B.** Sprite
**C.** Root beer
**D.** Pepsi

**9.** How does the McAllister's house lose power?

**A.** A big snow storm hits
**B.** A tree falls over and hits an electrical wire
**C.** A robber cuts off the power to their home
**D.** The electric company shuts off the power because they forgot to pay their bill

# ANSWERS

· · · · · · · · · · · · · · · · · · · · · · · · · · · · · · · · · · ·

**7.**    **B.**    For his family to disappear

**8.**    **D.**    Pepsi

**9.**    **B.**    A tree falls over and hits an electrical wire

**10.** When does Kate, Kevin's mom, realize Kevin is missing?

    **A.** On the way to the airport
    **B.** On the airplane
    **C.** Once she is in Paris
    **D.** She never realizes it

**11.** What does Kevin accidentally shoplift?

    **A.** A frozen pizza
    **B.** A bag of marbles
    **C.** Cleaning supplies for the home
    **D.** A toothbrush

**12.** With whom does Kate hitch a ride back to Chicago once she is back in the U.S.?

    **A.** A polka band
    **B.** A children's choir
    **C.** An alternative punk band
    **D.** A folk duo and their singing horse

**13.** What does Marv step in on the basement steps that causes him to lose his shoe?

    **A.** Tar
    **B.** Chewing gum
    **C.** Molasses
    **D.** Superglue

# ANSWERS

. . . . . . . . . . . . . . . . . . . . . . . . . . . . . . . . . . . . .

**10.**   **B.**   On the airplane

**11.**   **D.**   A toothbrush

**12.**   **A.**   A polka band

**13.**   **A.**   Tar

**14.** What movie does the McAllister family watch in Paris?

    **A.** *Gremlins*
    **B.** *It's a Wonderful Life*
    **C.** *White Christmas*
    **D.** *The Grinch*

**15.** Where does Gus, the leader of the polka band, tell Kate he once accidentally left his kids?

    **A.** The mall
    **B.** A car wash
    **C.** Ohio
    **D.** A funeral parlor

**16.** Who saves Kevin from the bandits' wrath?

    **A.** His mom
    **B.** Buzz
    **C.** Old Man Marley
    **D.** Mr. Murphy

## ANSWERS

**14.**     **B.**     *It's a Wonderful Life*

**15.**     **D.**     A funeral parlor

**16.**     **C.**     Old Man Marley

**17.  TRUE OR FALSE:**

The character of Gus Pulanski was based on a real-life "Polka King."

**18.  TRUE OR FALSE:**

*Home Alone* was only overtaken as the highest-grossing live action comedy by *The Hangover.*

**19.  TRUE OR FALSE:**

*Home Alone* has three sequels.

**20.  TRUE OR FALSE:**

John Candy improvised all of his lines.

# ANSWERS

.........................................

**17.** **TRUE**

**18.** **FALSE:** It was overtaken by *The Hangover Part II*.

**19.** **FALSE:** It has four sequels.

**20.** **TRUE**

# Home Alone 2: Lost in New York

1. What year did *Home Alone 2: Lost in New York* come out?

   **A.** 1992
   **B.** 1993
   **C.** 1994
   **D.** 1995

2. Where does the McCallister family decide to go on vacation?

   **A.** Paris
   **B.** Los Angeles
   **C.** New York
   **D.** Miami

## ANSWERS

......................................

**1.** **A.** 1992

**2.** **D.** Miami

**3.** Why does Kevin not want to go on his family's vacation?

   **A.** He is worried his home will get broken into again

   **B.** He would rather go to Paris because he missed out on it last year

   **C.** There aren't any Christmas trees in Florida

   **D.** He hates his family

**4.** Kevin accidentally boards a plane headed for where?

   **A.** Paris

   **B.** Los Angeles

   **C.** New York

   **D.** Miami

**5.** What does Kevin stop to buy in the airport that causes him to get separated from his family?

   **A.** Candy

   **B.** Batteries

   **C.** A magazine

   **D.** Pizza

## ANSWERS

· · · · · · · · · · · · · · · · · · · · · · · · · · · · · · · · · · · · ·

**3.**    **C.**    There aren't any Christmas trees in Florida

**4.**    **C.**    New York

**5.**    **B.**    Batteries

**6.** What happens to Kate when she realizes Kevin is not with the family?

    **A.** She throws up
    **B.** She laughs
    **C.** She cries
    **D.** She faints

**7.** How does Kevin have the funds to check into the Plaza Hotel?

    **A.** He sneaks into a room
    **B.** He steals a tip jar from a restaurant
    **C.** He dances on the sidewalk for money
    **D.** He uses his father's credit card

**8.** What is the name of the toy store Kevin goes to?

    **A.** Gimbels
    **B.** Harvey's Treasure's
    **C.** Duncan's Toy Chest
    **D.** Toy Island

# ANSWERS

· · · · · · · · · · · · · · · · · · · · · · · · · · · · · · · · · · · · · · · · · · · ·

**6.**    **D.**    She faints

**7.**    **D.**    He uses his father's credit card

**8.**    **C.**    Duncan's Toy Chest

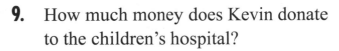

**9.** How much money does Kevin donate to the children's hospital?

    **A.** $20
    **B.** $30
    **C.** $40
    **D.** $50

**10.** Who does Kevin run into in New York?

    **A.** His family
    **B.** Old Man Marley
    **C.** The burglars from *Home Alone*
    **D.** His best friend, Michael

**11.** Where do the burglars plan on robbing?

    **A.** The toy store
    **B.** The children's hospital
    **C.** The Plaza Hotel
    **D.** Saks Fifth Avenue

# ANSWERS

· · · · · · · · · · · · · · · · · · · · · · · · · · · · · · · · · · · · ·

**9.**    **A.**    $20

**10.**    **C.**    The burglars from *Home Alone*

**11.**    **A.**    The toy store

**12.** Who does Kevin befriend in Central Park?

    **A.** A prostitute

    **B.** The owner of the toy store

    **C.** A lady he saw earlier in the film feeding pigeons

    **D.** A street performer

**13.** How does Kevin get saved from the bandits, who end up catching him?

    **A.** He kicks them in the shin

    **B.** The Pigeon Lady throws bird seed at them and they are attacked by pigeons

    **C.** He pummels them with ornaments from the Rockefeller Center Christmas tree

    **D.** He blinds them with the flash of a camera

**14.** Where does Kate eventually find Kevin?

    **A.** Central Park

    **B.** Times Sqaure

    **C.** The Rockefeller Center

    **D.** Fifth Avenue

# ANSWERS

. . . . . . . . . . . . . . . . . . . . . . . . . . . . . . . . . . . .

**12.** **C.** A lady he saw earlier in the film feeding pigeons

**13.** **B.** The Pigeon Lady throws bird seed at them and they are attacked by pigeons

**14.** **C.** The Rockefeller Center

**15.** What does Kevin give to the Pigeon Lady as a gesture of friendship?

**A.** A candy cane

**B.** A porcelain turtle dove ornament

**C.** A novelty tin of Chicago-style popcorn

**D.** A letter saying she is always welcome to come visit him

**16.** How does the movie end?

**A.** With the McCallisters agreeing that they will never go on vacation again

**B.** With the bandits going to prison

**C.** With the pigeon lady marrying the owner of the toy store

**D.** With Kevin's dad yelling about the room service bill

# ANSWERS

· · · · · · · · · · · · · · · · · · · · · · · · · · · · · · · · · · · · · · ·

**15.** **B.** A porcelain turtle dove ornament

**16.** **D.** With Kevin's dad yelling about the room service bill

**17. TRUE OR FALSE:**

The film was the second most financially successful film of 1992.

**18. TRUE OR FALSE:**

This was the only *Home Alone* sequel featuring the original cast.

**19. TRUE OR FALSE:**

In *Home Alone 2,* Kevin once again watches the film *Angels with Filthy Souls*.

**20. TRUE OR FALSE:**

Kevin stops to buy batteries for his Walkman.

**21. TRUE OR FALSE:**

The McCallisters almost miss their flight once again due to a power outage.

## ANSWERS

. . . . . . . . . . . . . . . . . . . . . . . . . . . . . . . . . . . . . .

**17.**     **TRUE**

**18.**     **TRUE**

**19.**     **FALSE:** He watches a film called *Angels with Even Filthier Souls.*

**20.**     **FALSE:** He stops to buy batteries for his Talkboy.

**21.**     **FALSE:** They almost miss their flight because Peter accidentally unplugs his alarm clock.

# *Gremlins*

**1.** When was *Gremlins* released?

    **A.** 1982
    **B.** 1983
    **C.** 1984
    **D.** 1985

**2.** Who was the executive producer of the film and also appears in a brief cameo?

    **A.** John Hughes
    **B.** George Lucas
    **C.** Steven Spielberg
    **D.** James Cameron

**3.** What is the profession of Randall Peltzer?

    **A.** Librarian
    **B.** Artist
    **C.** Bus driver
    **D.** Inventor

· · · · · · · · · · · · · · · · · · · · · · · · · · · · · · · · · ·

**1.** **C.** 1984

**2.** **C.** Steven Spielberg

**3.** **D.** Inventor

**4.** Where does Randall Peltzer first encounter the mogwai?

    **A.** Chinatown
    **B.** Queens
    **C.** The Upper East Side
    **D.** In the New York City Subway

**5.** Why does Mr. Wing's grandson secretly sell the mogwai to Randall?

    **A.** He wants to see Randall suffer
    **B.** His family needs the money
    **C.** He is sick of being the only one who takes care of the mogwai
    **D.** The mogwai is his mean older brother's favorite pet and he wants to get revenge on his brother

**6.** Which is NOT a rule in caring for the mogwai?

    **A.** Don't give it a name
    **B.** Don't let it near bright light
    **C.** Don't let it touch water
    **D.** Don't feed it after midnight

## ANSWERS

· · · · · · · · · · · · · · · · · · · · · · · · · · · · · · · · · · · · · ·

**4.**   **A.**   Chinatown

**5.**   **B.**   His family needs the money

**6.**   **A.**   Don't give it a name

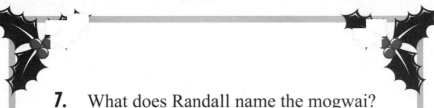

**7.** What does Randall name the mogwai?

    **A.** Gizmo
    **B.** Gadget
    **C.** Gremlin
    **D.** Gary

**8.** What happens when Billy's friend spills water on the mogwai?

    **A.** It gets bigger
    **B.** It multiplies
    **C.** It turns evil
    **D.** Its eyes turn red

**9.** How does the mogwai obtain food after midnight?

    **A.** It sneaks into the fridge
    **B.** It has been hoarding food since morning
    **C.** Billy feeds it to see what happens
    **D.** The science teacher leaves food out

. . . . . . . . . . . . . . . . . . . . . . . . . . . . . . . . . . . . . . . . . .

**7.**   **A.**   Gizmo

**8.**   **B.**   It multiplies

**9.**   **D.**   The science teacher leaves food out

**10.** What happens to the mogwais after they emerge from their cocoons?

    **A.** They turn into butterflies

    **B.** They turn into Gremlins

    **C.** They die

    **D.** They get nicer

**11.** Which is NOT a way in which Billy's mother kills Gremlins?

    **A.** Killing one in a blender

    **B.** Stabbing one with a knife

    **C.** Running over one with a lawnmower

    **D.** Blowing one up in the microwave

**12.** How does the only remaining Gremlin multiply?

    **A.** It jumps in a swimming pool

    **B.** It jumps in a lake

    **C.** It drinks a whole fish tank worth of water

    **D.** It eats an entire Chinese buffet

## ANSWERS

. . . . . . . . . . . . . . . . . . . . . . . . . . . . . . . . . . . . . . .

**10.** **B.** They turn into Gremlins

**11.** **C.** Running over one with a lawnmower

**12.** **A.** It jumps in a swimming pool

**13.** How does Kate first realize the Gremlins are afraid of light?

    **A.** She turns the lights on in the bar

    **B.** She takes a picture of them and the camera flash frightens them

    **C.** The police come and their sirens scare them

    **D.** She tries to light a cigarette

**14.** Why does Kate dislike Christmas?

    **A.** She is sickened by the consumerism it promotes

    **B.** Once on Christmas Eve she got locked out of her house and had to sleep in the cold

    **C.** Her father died on Christmas Eve

    **D.** Her grandmother once choked on a Christmas cookie

**15.** What movie do Billy and Kate find the gremlins watching?

    **A.** *Cinderella*

    **B.** *Snow White*

    **C.** *Sleeping Beauty*

    **D.** *Alice in Wonderland*

# ANSWERS

· · · · · · · · · · · · · · · · · · · · · · · · · · · · · · · · · · · ·

**13.** **D.** She tries to light a cigarette

**14.** **C.** Her father died on Christmas Eve

**15.** **B.** *Snow White*

**16.** Billy and Kate blow up most of the Gremlins in the movie theater. However, one remains. What happens to the remaining Gremlin when it is exposed to sunlight?

- **A.** It reproduces again
- **B.** It explodes
- **C.** It screams
- **D.** It melts into a puddle

**17. TRUE OR FALSE:**

The violent content in *Gremlins* was part of the reason the Motion Picture Association of America altered its rating system.

**18. TRUE OR FALSE:**

Howard Stern provides the voice of Gizmo to mogwai.

**19. TRUE OR FALSE:**

The idea of Gremlin monsters was a completely original idea.

## ANSWERS

········································

**16.** **D.** It melts into a puddle

**17.** **TRUE**

**18.** **FALSE:** Howie Mandel provides the voice of Gizmo.

**19.** **FALSE:** Gremlins are loosely based on a joke during WWII that aircraft failure could be blamed on small monsters called Gremlins. They were also the subject of a 1943 book by Roald Dahl.

## 20. TRUE OR FALSE:

The word *mogwai* is Cantonese for *monster.*

## 21. TRUE OR FALSE:

*Gremlins* was the highest grossing film of 1984.

## 22. TRUE OR FALSE:

Kate's dad died in a car crash on Christmas Eve.

## 23. TRUE OR FALSE:

The Peltzer family never sees Mr. Wing again.

## 24. TRUE OR FALSE:

All the monsters in the movie die.

## ANSWERS

. . . . . . . . . . . . . . . . . . . . . . . . . . . . . . . . . . . . . . . . .

**20.**  **TRUE**

**21.**  **FALSE:**  It was the fourth highest grossing film of the year.

**22.**  **FALSE:**  He died because he got stuck in the chimney while dressed as Santa.

**23.**  **FALSE:**  Mr. Wing confronts them at the end of the movie and expresses his disgust with them.

**24.**  **FALSE:**  Gizmo, the original mogwai, survives and is taken back by Mr. Wing

# Miracle on 34th Street

**1.** What year was *Miracle on 34th Street* released?
- **A.** 1945
- **B.** 1946
- **C.** 1947
- **D.** 1948

**2.** Who plays the role of Kris Kringle?
- **A.** Edmund Gwenn
- **B.** John Payne
- **C.** George Seaton
- **D.** Donald Crisp

**3.** Which child star plays the role of Susan?
- **A.** Shirley Temple
- **B.** Karolyn Grimes
- **C.** Darla Hood
- **D.** Natalie Wood

## ANSWERS

......................................

**1.** **B.** 1946

**2.** **A.** Edmund Gwenn

**3.** **D.** Natalie Wood

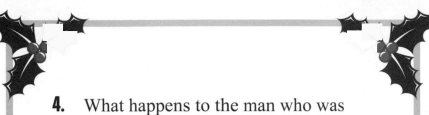

**4.** What happens to the man who was originally supposed to play Santa in the Thanksgiving Day Parade?

    **A.** He is hit by a car
    **B.** He oversleeps his alarm
    **C.** He is too drunk
    **D.** He elopes to Atlantic City

**5.** What store is Kris Kringle hired to play Santa at?

    **A.** Macy's
    **B.** Gimbel's
    **C.** Lord & Taylor
    **D.** Saks Fifth Avenue

**6.** Why does Doris fire Kris?

    **A.** He directs customers to competitor stores
    **B.** He yells at a child
    **C.** He tells Doris's daughter, Susan, that he is the real Santa
    **D.** He shoplifts from the toy department

. . . . . . . . . . . . . . . . . . . . . . . . . . . . . . . .

**4.**    **C.**    He is too drunk

**5.**    **A.**    Macy's

**6.**    **C.**    He tells Doris's daughter,
Susan, that he is the real Santa

7. What language does Doris hear Kris speaking with a young orphan?

    **A.** French

    **B.** Spanish

    **C.** Swedish

    **D.** Dutch

8. What does Kris promise Susan for Christmas?

    **A.** A house

    **B.** A car

    **C.** A pony

    **D.** A record player

9. Why does Kris get confined to a mental hospital?

    **A.** He keeps insisting that he is the real Santa

    **B.** He yells at a child in the middle of the store

    **C.** He hits Granville Sawyer with an umbrella

    **D.** He lies to Susan about being able to give her what she wants for Christmas

# ANSWERS

........................................

**7.**    **D.**   Dutch

**8.**    **A.**   A house

**9.**    **C.**   He hits Granville Sawyer with an umbrella

**10.** What does Mr. Macy say when Fred asks him in court if he believes in Santa?

    **A.** "Of course not!"

    **B.** "You bet!"

    **C.** "I do."

    **D.** "Is that a serious question?"

**11.** What causes Judge Harper to dismiss the case?

    **A.** The Post Office formally recognizes Kris as Santa

    **B.** A group of children attests in court that Kris is the real Santa

    **C.** Kris performs magic in front of the court

    **D.** Judge Harper realizes the case is silly and a waste of time

**12.** Why does Kris not accept Doris's dinner invitation?

    **A.** Santa cannot eat regular human food

    **B.** It's Christmas Eve

    **C.** He made other plans

    **D.** He is too exhausted from being in a court battle all day

# ANSWERS

. . . . . . . . . . . . . . . . . . . . . . . . . . . . . . . . . . .

**10.**   **C.**   "I do."

**11.**   **A.**   The Post Office formally recognizes Kris as Santa

**12.**   **B.**   It's Christmas Eve

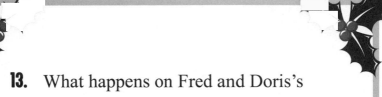

**13.** What happens on Fred and Doris's drive home?

    **A.** They get in a car crash

    **B.** They see Santa flying over them in his sleigh

    **C.** They find a stray reindeer

    **D.** They see the house of Susan's dreams up for sale

**14.** Why does Fred think he must be a great lawyer?

    **A.** He got Kris out of the mental institution

    **B.** He proved that Kris was Santa

    **C.** He negotiated Kris's bail down

    **D.** He found a legal error in the lease of the home he wants to buy

**15.** What does Fred notice leaning up against the fireplace in the house?

    **A.** An umbrella

    **B.** The sled that he had always dreamed of getting for Christmas when he was a child

    **C.** Kris's cane

    **D.** A pair of Santa's boots

# ANSWERS

· · · · · · · · · · · · · · · · · · · · · · · · · · · · · · · · · · · · · · ·

**13.** **D.** They see the house of Susan's dreams up for sale

**14.** **B.** He proved that Kris was Santa

**15.** **C.** Kris's cane

**16. TRUE OR FALSE:**

The rival between Macy's and Gimbels in the movie is based on a real-life rivalry.

**17. TRUE OR FALSE:**

John Hughes made a remake of the film in 1994.

**18. TRUE OR FALSE:**

The titular street, 34th Street, refers to the street on which the house at the end is located.

**19. TRUE OR FALSE:**

*Miracle on 34th Street* was the first full-length black-and-white film to be colorized.

**20. TRUE OR FALSE:**

*Miracle on 34th Street* won the Academy Award for Best Picture.

. . . . . . . . . . . . . . . . . . . . . . . . . . . . . . . . . . .

**16.** **TRUE**

**17.** **TRUE**

**18.** **FALSE:** It refers to the location of the Macy's flagship store in New York City.

**19.** **TRUE**

**20.** **FALSE:** The film won Academy Awards for Best Actor in a Supporting Role; Best Writing, Original Story; and Best Writing, Screenplay. It lost Best Picture to *Gentleman's Agreement*.

**21. TRUE OR FALSE:**

The movie was the first Christmas film released by 20th Century Fox.

**22. TRUE OR FALSE:**

Although it's a Christmas movie, *Miracle on 34th Street* was released in May.

**23. TRUE OR FALSE:**

In the 1994 remake, instead of communicating with the little girl in Dutch, Kringle communicates with her in Spanish.

**24. TRUE OR FALSE:**

When Kris tells a customer that a competing store has better deals, Macy's loses out on a lot of business.

## ANSWERS

· · · · · · · · · · · · · · · · · · · · · · · · · · · · · · · · · ·

**21.** **TRUE**

**22.** **TRUE**

**23.** **FALSE:** He communicates with her in sign language.

**24.** **FALSE:** The woman is so impressed with Kris's honesty that she pledges to be a loyal customer to Macy's.

# Planes, Trains and Automobiles

1. What year was the movie released?
    - **A.** 1986
    - **B.** 1987
    - **C.** 1988
    - **D.** 1989

2. Who wrote and directed the film?
    - **A.** John Hughes
    - **B.** Chris Columbus
    - **C.** Steve Martin
    - **D.** Steven Soderbergh

# ANSWERS

· · · · · · · · · · · · · · · · · · · · · · · · · · · · · · · · · · · · ·

**1.**   **B.**   1987

**2.**   **A.**   John Hughes

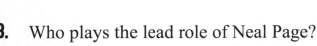

**3.** Who plays the lead role of Neal Page?

    **A.** Alec Baldwin

    **B.** Will Ferrell

    **C.** John Candy

    **D.** Steve Martin

**4.** What sort of salesman is Del Griffith?

    **A.** A mattress salesman

    **B.** A toothpick salesman

    **C.** A shower curtain ring salesman

    **D.** A high-tech toaster salesman

**5.** To where is Neal traveling in the movie?

    **A.** Chicago

    **B.** New York City

    **C.** Milwaukee

    **D.** Kansas City

**6.** Where is the plane out of La Guardia diverted?

    **A.** Oklahoma City

    **B.** St. Louis

    **C.** Topeka

    **D.** Wichita

........................................................

**3.** **D.** Steve Martin

**4.** **C.** A shower curtain ring salesman

**5.** **A.** Chicago

**6.** **D.** Wichita

7. What happens when Neal and Del are sleeping in their motel?
   A. There is a fire at the motel
   B. A car drives through their first-floor window
   C. Cockroaches infiltrate
   D. A burglar steals their cash

8. When the train breaks down, where are the men stranded?
   A. In the desert
   B. In a field in Missouri
   C. In an abandoned mining town
   D. In a suburb of Chicago

9. What does Del sell in Jefferson City to obtain money for bus tickets?
   A. His soul
   B. His shoes
   C. His remaining shower curtain rings
   D. A box of antique photographs that his grandmother gave him

## ANSWERS

........................................

**7.**    **D.**    A burglar steals their cash

**8.**    **B.**    In a field in Missouri

**9.**    **C.**    His remaining shower curtain rings

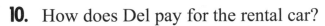

**10.** How does Del pay for the rental car?

    **A.**  He finds a bag of money on the side of the road

    **B.**  With Neal's credit card

    **C.**  He steals the car

    **D.**  He robs a local diner

**11.** How does Neal lose his credit card?

    **A.**  It is destroyed in the car fire

    **B.**  It blows away in a strong gust of wind

    **C.**  A pigeon swoops down and snatches it out of his hand

    **D.**  A geomagnetic storm ruins the magnetic strip on it

**12.** How does the duo finally make it back to Chicago?

    **A.**  In the back of a chicken truck

    **B.**  In the back of a tomato truck

    **C.**  In the back of a refrigerator truck

    **D.**  In the back of a shower curtain ring truck

## ANSWERS

· · · · · · · · · · · · · · · · · · · · · · · · · · · · · · · · · · · · ·

**10.** **B.** With Neal's credit card

**11.** **A.** It is destroyed in the car fire

**12.** **C.** In the back of a refrigerator truck

**13.** Neal and Del part ways at the train station in Chicago. However, Neal then decides to return to the station. What does Neal find when he returns to the train station in Chicago?

**A.** Luggage that he forgot

**B.** His family waiting for him

**C.** Del sitting alone with nowhere to go on Thanksgiving

**D.** The money that was stolen from him earlier in the movie

**14.** How long has Del's wife been dead?

**A.** One year

**B.** Three years

**C.** Eight ycars

**D.** Ten years

**15.** How does Del end up spending his Thanksgiving?

**A.** Alone at the train station

**B.** Sitting with Neal at the train station

**C.** Visiting his dead wife's grave

**D.** At Neal's home with Neal's family

# ANSWERS

............................................

**13.**   **C.**   Del sitting alone with nowhere to go on Thanksgiving

**14.**   **C.**   Eight years

**15.**   **D.**   At Neal's home with Neal's family

## 16. TRUE OR FALSE:

In Steve Martin's scene ranting to the rental car company, he says the F-word 15 times.

## 17. TRUE OR FALSE:

*Plane, Trains and Automobiles* is often considered one of John Candy's best films.

## 18. TRUE OR FALSE:

John Hughes was inspired by an actual flight he was on from New York to Chicago that got diverted to Wichita.

## 19. TRUE OR FALSE:

This film is featured in Roger Ebert's Great Movies collection.

# ANSWERS

...............................................

**16.** **FALSE:** He says it 18 times.

**17.** **TRUE**

**18.** **TRUE**

**19.** **TRUE**

### 20. TRUE OR FALSE:

The production team had to pay transportation companies over $3 million in order to use their names and logos in the film.

### 21. TRUE OR FALSE:

Neal and Del's journey takes five days.

### 22. TRUE OR FALSE:

Kevin Bacon has a cameo role in the film.

### 23. TRUE OR FALSE:

Neal works as an advertising executive.

### 24. TRUE OR FALSE:

*Planes, Trains and Automobiles* is often considered one of the best comedies of all time.

## ANSWERS

. . . . . . . . . . . . . . . . . . . . . . . . . . . . . . . . . . . . . .

**20. FALSE:** No transportations companies wanted to be associated with poor service in the film, so all of the companies are made up.

**21. FALSE:** It takes three days.

**22. TRUE**

**23. TRUE**

**24. TRUE**

# The Shop Around the Corner

1. What year was *The Shop Around the Corner* released?

    **A.** 1940
    **B.** 1941
    **C.** 1942
    **D.** 1943

2. The film takes place in the years leading up to which war?

    **A.** The Civil War
    **B.** The Russian Civil War
    **C.** World War I
    **D.** World War II

# ANSWERS

· · · · · · · · · · · · · · · · · · · · · · · · · · · · · · · · · · ·

**1.** **A.** 1940

**2.** **D.** World War II

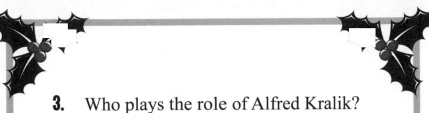

**3.** Who plays the role of Alfred Kralik?

    **A.** Cary Grant

    **B.** John Wayne

    **C.** James Stewart

    **D.** Clark Gable

**4.** In what city does the film take place?

    **A.** Prague

    **B.** Bucharest

    **C.** Vienna

    **D.** Budapest

**5.** What causes Mr. Matuschek to hire Klara?

    **A.** She successfully sells a cigarette box

    **B.** She is so beautiful he thinks she will bring business

    **C.** She is his brother's daughter and he owes his brother a favor

    **D.** She compliments Mr. Matuschek's tie that Alfred has just insulted

## ANSWERS

........................................

**3.** **C.** James Stewart

**4.** **D.** Budapest

**5.** **A.** She successfully sells a
cigarette box

**6.** Who has Alfred secretly been corresponding with?

    **A.** The widow of his late brother

    **B.** His childhood sweetheart

    **C.** A woman whose ad he came across in the newspaper

    **D.** A woman who works at a competitor store of Mr. Matuschek

**7.** Who plays the role of Klara?

    **A.** Judy Garland

    **B.** Maureen O'Sullivan

    **C.** Margaret Sullavan

    **D.** Grace Kelly

**8.** Why does Mr. Matuschek fire Alfred?

    **A.** Alfred is a bad employee

    **B.** Mr. Matuschek thinks Alfred is having an affair with his wife

    **C.** Mr. Matuschek thinks Alfred and Klara are flirting, and Matuschek has a crush on Klara himself

    **D.** Alfred was framed for stealing money from the cash register

# ANSWERS

......................................

**6.** **C.** A woman whose ad he came across in the newspaper

**7.** **C.** Margaret Sullavan

**8.** **B.** Mr. Matuschek thinks Alfred is having an affair with his wife

9. Who does Alfred's mystery woman end up being?

    **A.** Klara

    **B.** Mr. Matuschek's wife

    **C.** Alfred's own sister

    **D.** A beautiful woman he always sees pass by the store

10. What does Alfred do when he sees who the mystery woman is?

    **A.** He proposes to her

    **B.** He doesn't tell her that he is the mystery man, and she tells him to go away

    **C.** He yells at her in front of the entire café for tricking him

    **D.** He pretends to be sick and then leaves

11. Why is Mr. Matuschek in the hospital?

    **A.** He had a heart attack

    **B.** He got hit by a streetcar

    **C.** He broke his leg after slipping on an icy sidewalk

    **D.** He attempted to commit suicide

· · · · · · · · · · · · · · · · · · · · · · · · · · · · · · · · · · · · · · · · · · · · · · ·

**9.**   **A.**   Klara

**10.**   **B.**   He doesn't tell her that he is the mystery man, and she tells him to go away

**11.**   **D.**   He attempted to commit suicide

**12.** What happens to the store's sales on Christmas Eve?

    **A.** They plummet and the store must close its doors

    **B.** They reach record highs and Mr. Matuschek gives everyone a bonus

    **C.** They fall, but Klara goes onto the streets to advertise their goods, and sales eventually pick up again

    **D.** They fall, but an anonymous donor steps in to make sure they don't have to close their doors

**13.** How does Alfred reveal to Klara that he is the man with whom she has been corresponding?

    **A.** He explains it in a letter

    **B.** He asks Mr. Matuschek to tell her

    **C.** He pins a carnation, the flower they agreed would be their signal, to his lapel

    **D.** He brings up a secret that she disclosed to him in a letter

## ANSWERS

**12.** **B.** They reach record highs and Mr. Matuschek gives everyone a bonus

**13.** **C.** He pins a carnation, the flower they agreed would be their signal, to his lapel

**14.** What 1990s film references *The Shop Around the Corner?*

    **A.** *You've Got Mail*
    **B.** *Sleepless in Seattle*
    **C.** *Notting Hill*
    **D.** *My Best Friend's Wedding*

**15. TRUE OR FALSE:**

*The Shop Around the Corner* was based on a play of the same name.

**16. TRUE OR FALSE:**

The film had a budget of only $500,000.

**17. TRUE OR FALSE:**

*The Shop Around the Corner* is often considered one of the best films ever made.

**18. TRUE OR FALSE:**

Stewart and Sullavan first met on the day they filmed their first scene together.

· · · · · · · · · · · · · · · · · · · · · · · · · · · · · · · · · · · · · · ·

**14.** **A.** 1990

**15.** **FALSE:** It was based on a play called *Parfumerie.*

**16.** **TRUE**

**17.** **TRUE**

**18.** **FALSE:** They met long before making the movie, and Stewart followed Sullavan to New York to start his acting career.

# Mixed Nuts

1. What year was *Mixed Nuts* released?
   - **A.** 1992
   - **B.** 1993
   - **C.** 1994
   - **D.** 1995

2. What director of movies such as *You've Got Mail* and *Sleepless in Seattle* directed *Mixed Nuts?*
   - **A.** Rob Reiner
   - **B.** Nora Ephron
   - **C.** Peter Segal
   - **D.** Sofia Coppola

## ANSWERS

**1.**  **C.**  1994

**2.**  **B.**  Nora Ephron

**3.** When does the film begin?

    **A.** Christmas Eve

    **B.** Christmas Day

    **C.** New Year's Eve

    **D.** Three weeks before Christmas

**4.** Who plays the role of Philip?

    **A.** John Candy

    **B.** Adam Sandler

    **C.** Billy Crystal

    **D.** Steve Martin

**5.** What is the name of the suicide-prevention hotline run by Philip?

    **A.** Not Too Late

    **B.** Crisis Care

    **C.** Lifesavers

    **D.** Saving Grace

**6.** What is the name of the serial killer on the loose in Los Angeles?

    **A.** The California Killer

    **B.** The Desert Decapitator

    **C.** The Seaside Strangler

    **D.** The Hollywood Horror Man

# ANSWERS

....................................................

**3.** **A.** Christmas Eve

**4.** **D.** Steve Martin

**5.** **C.** Lifesavers

**6.** **C.** The Seaside Strangler

**7.** Why is the landlord evicting Philip and the crisis hotline?

    **A.** He thinks having a suicide-prevention hotline in his building gives people the wrong message

    **B.** The employees are loud and disrespectful

    **C.** He is refurbishing the building to turn it into luxury condos

    **D.** Philip cannot pay rent

**8.** What happens when Philip asks his girlfriend, Susan, for a loan?

    **A.** She says no

    **B.** She tells him she has been dating someone else

    **C.** She breaks up with Philip

    **D.** All of the above

**9.** What does Gracie throw at Felix that causes a large cut on his forehead?

    **A.** A Christmas ornament

    **B.** A fruitcake

    **C.** A stale gingerbread cookie

    **D.** A knife she had been using to spread frosting on Christmas cookies

# ANSWERS

· · · · · · · · · · · · · · · · · · · · · · · · · · · · · · · · · · · · · · ·

**7.** **D.** Philip cannot pay rent

**8.** **D.** All of the above

**9.** **B.** A fruitcake

**10.** Where do Philip and Catherine take Felix to be treated for his head wound?

   **A.** A pediatrician

   **B.** A dentist

   **C.** A veterinarian

   **D.** A high school anatomy teacher

**11.** How does Felix end up in the hospital?

   **A.** He steals dog tranquilizers and overdoses on them

   **B.** His head wound is much more serious than anyone initially thought

   **C.** He slips on a wet floor and breaks his wrist

   **D.** His friends think he tried to kill himself

**12.** What does Mrs. Munchnik threaten to sue Philip for?

   **A.** Withholding information about being evicted

   **B.** Withholding wages

   **C.** Inappropriate office behavior

   **D.** Both A and C

**10.**    **C.**    A veterinarian

**11.**    **A.**    He steals dog tranquilizers and overdoses on them

**12.**    **D.**    Both A and C

**13.** Who accidentally kills Stanley?

    **A.** Gracie

    **B.** Chris

    **C.** Philip

    **D.** Mrs. Munchnik

**14.** What do Gracie and Felix disguise Stanley's body as?

    **A.** An animatronic Santa

    **B.** A moose carcass

    **C.** A Christmas tree

    **D.** A box of restaurant supplies

**15.** What do the police find in Stanley's bag?

    **A.** Drugs

    **B.** Evidence that he is the Seaside Strangler

    **C.** Stolen Christmas presents

    **D.** Fake eviction notices he was giving to all of his tenants in order to trick them into paying higher rent

# ANSWERS

. . . . . . . . . . . . . . . . . . . . . . . . . . . . . . . . . . . . . . .

**13.** **A.** Gracie

**14.** **C.** A Christmas tree

**15.** **B.** Evidence that he is the Seaside Strangler

**16. TRUE OR FALSE:**

*Mixed Nuts* was based on a French film.

**17. TRUE OR FALSE:**

This was Liev Schreiber's first film role.

**18. TRUE OR FALSE:**

*Mixed Nuts* was a commercial and critical success.

**19. TRUE OR FALSE:**

Gracie goes to jail for killing Stanley.

## ANSWERS

· · · · · · · · · · · · · · · · · · · · · · · · · · · · · · · · · · · · · ·

**16.** **TRUE**

**17.** **TRUE**

**18.** **FALSE:** It received largely negative reviews and did not even gross $7 million by the end of its run at the box office.

**19.** **FALSE:** She is awarded $250,000 for killing the Seaside Strangler.

**1.** What year was *Elf* released?

    **A.** 2002

    **B.** 2003

    **C.** 2004

    **D.** 2005

**2.** Who plays the role of Buddy the Elf?

    **A.** Steve Martin

    **B.** Ben Stiller

    **C.** John C. Reilly

    **D.** Will Ferrell

· · · · · · · · · · · · · · · · · · · · · · · · · · · · · · · · · · ·

**1.**   **B.**   2003

**2.**   **D.**   Will Ferrell

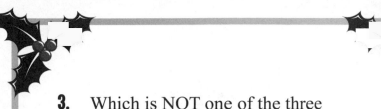

**3.** Which is NOT one of the three professions available to elves?

    **A.** Being a shoe cobbler
    **B.** Asking riddles to travelers going over bridges
    **C.** Baking cookies in trees
    **D.** Building toys in Santa's workshop

**4.** Why do the elves name the baby Buddy?

    **A.** He is wearing "Little Buddy Diapers"
    **B.** Buddy is their favorite name
    **C.** They think of him as their buddy
    **D.** Since he is a baby, they associate him with a budding plant

**5.** What elf job is Buddy demoted to when he cannot adequately make toys?

    **A.** Cleaning up after the reindeer
    **B.** Toy testing
    **C.** Polishing Santa's sleigh
    **D.** Snow plowing

# ANSWERS

· · · · · · · · · · · · · · · · · · · · · · · · · · · · · · · · · · · ·

**3.**    **B.**    Asking riddles to travelers going over bridges

**4.**    **A.**    He is wearing "Little Buddy Diapers"

**5.**    **B.**    Toy testing

**6.** What happened to Buddy's birth mother?

    **A.** She moved to Paris
    **B.** She mysteriously disappeared
    **C.** She started a new family
    **D.** She died

**7.** What is the profession of Buddy's dad, Walter?

    **A.** Advertising executive
    **B.** Talent agent
    **C.** Children's book publisher
    **D.** Editor in Chief of a magazine

**8.** What is Buddy shocked to learn about Walter?

    **A.** He has a terminal illness
    **B.** He is a billionaire
    **C.** He has seventeen other kids
    **D.** He is on the Naughty List

# ANSWERS

. . . . . . . . . . . . . . . . . . . . . . . . . . . . . . . . . . . . . . . . .

**6.**    **D.**    She died

**7.**    **C.**    Children's book publisher

**8.**    **D.**    He is on the Naughty List

**9.** At what store does Buddy get a job as an elf?

    **A.** Gimbel's

    **B.** Macy's

    **C.** Saks Fifth Avenue

    **D.** Lord & Taylor

**10.** What does Buddy tell the mall Santa he smells like?

    **A.** Soup

    **B.** Stale M&Ms

    **C.** Beef and cheese

    **D.** Lies

**11.** What does Buddy cat at the doctor's office?

    **A.** Tongue depressors

    **B.** Cotton swabs

    **C.** Cotton balls

    **D.** Latex gloves

# ANSWERS

. . . . . . . . . . . . . . . . . . . . . . . . . . . . . . . . . . . . . . . .

**9.**    **A.**    Gimbel's

**10.**    **C.**    Beef and cheese

**11.**    **C.**    Cotton balls

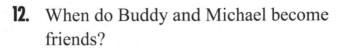

**12.** When do Buddy and Michael become friends?

    **A.** After they throw snowballs at bullies

    **B.** After Buddy gives Michael exactly what he wants for Christmas

    **C.** After Buddy lets Michael eat junk food for dinner

    **D.** After Buddy confronts Walter about being a bad father to Michael

**13.** When Buddy is in the mailroom, he gets drunk on whiskey because he thinks it's what?

    **A.** Christmas potion

    **B.** Maple syrup

    **C.** Melted chocolate

    **D.** Apple cider

**14.** Who plays the role of Jovie?

    **A.** Emily Blunt

    **B.** Anne Hathaway

    **C.** Rachel McAdams

    **D.** Zooey Deschanel

# ANSWERS

. . . . . . . . . . . . . . . . . . . . . . . . . . . . . . . . . . . . . . .

**12.**    **A.**    After they throw snowballs at bullies

**13.**    **B.**    Maple syrup

**14.**    **D.**    Zooey Deschanel

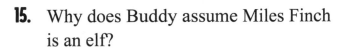

**15.** Why does Buddy assume Miles Finch is an elf?

    **A.** He is wearing green
    **B.** He is short in stature
    **C.** He has pointy shoes
    **D.** He speaks in rhymes

**16.** Where does Buddy write his note to Walter and his family?

    **A.** On a piece of Santa's stationary
    **B.** On the kitchen table, spelled out in pieces of candy
    **C.** With an Etch A Sketch
    **D.** He carves it in a block of Play-Doh

**17.** Where does Santa's sleigh crash?

    **A.** Central Park
    **B.** The Hudson River
    **C.** Times Square
    **D.** JFK Airport

# ANSWERS

........................................

**15.** **B.** He is short in stature

**16.** **C.** With an Etch A Sketch

**17.** **A.** Central Park

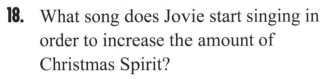

**18.** What song does Jovie start singing in order to increase the amount of Christmas Spirit?

    **A.** "Here Comes Santa Claus"
    **B.** "Jingle Bell Rock"
    **C.** "Santa Claus Is Coming to Town"
    **D.** "Santa Baby"

**19.** What does Walter eventually write a successful children's book about?

    **A.** Buddy's adventures in New York
    **B.** Working in corporate America
    **C.** Raising a nontraditional family
    **D.** Being on the Naughty List

**20.** What do Buddy and Jovie name their daughter?

    **A.** Caroline
    **B.** Kathy
    **C.** Susie
    **D.** Annie

# ANSWERS

· · · · · · · · · · · · · · · · · · · · · · · · · · · · · · · · · · · · ·

**18.** **C.** "Santa Claus Is Coming to Town"

**19.** **A.** Buddy's adventures in New York

**20.** **C.** Susie

### 21. TRUE OR FALSE:

Santa kidnaps Buddy from the orphanage.

### 22. TRUE OR FALSE:

Walter works in the iconic 30 Rockefeller Plaza building.

### 23. TRUE OR FALSE:

Michael is the one who encourages Buddy to ask Jovie on a date.

### 24. TRUE OR FALSE:

The role of Buddy the Elf was written for Will Ferrell.

### 25. TRUE OR FALSE:

There is a sequel to *Elf* called *Elf 2: Buddy Saves Christmas.*

## ANSWERS

. . . . . . . . . . . . . . . . . . . . . . . . . . . . . . . . . . . . . . . . . .

**21.**  **FALSE:**  Baby Buddy sneaks into Santa's bag to get a teddy bear.

**22.**  **FALSE:**  He works in the Empire State Building.

**23.**  **TRUE**

**24.**  **FALSE:**  Jim Carrey was the initial option to play Buddy.

**25.**  **FALSE:**  Jon Favreau wanted to make this sequel, but Will Ferrell would not sign on.

### 26. TRUE OR FALSE:

Director Jon Favreau provides the voice of Mr. Narwhal.

### 27. TRUE OR FALSE:

This was Will Ferrell's first movie role after leaving *Saturday Night Live*.

### 28. TRUE OR FALSE:

When Buddy is offered "fruit spray" at the mall, he uses it as cologne.

### 29. TRUE OR FALSE:

Buddy enters New York by the Brooklyn Bridge.

### 30. TRUE OR FALSE:

Will Ferrell had to actually eat all of the sugary food that Buddy the Elf eats in the movie.

## ANSWERS

· · · · · · · · · · · · · · · · · · · · · · · · · · · · · · · · · · · · · · · · · · ·

**26.** **TRUE**

**27.** **TRUE**

**28.** **FALSE:** He tries to eat the fruit spray.

**29.** **FALSE:** He walks through the Lincoln Tunnel to enter the city.

**30.** **TRUE**

## It's a Wonderful Life

1.  When did *It's a Wonderful Life* come out?

    **A.** 1943
    **B.** 1944
    **C.** 1945
    **D.** 1946

2.  What is the name of the town where the movie takes place?

    **A.** Saratoga Springs, New York
    **B.** Albany, New York
    **C.** Bedford Falls, New York
    **D.** Hudson, New York

## ANSWERS

·········································

**1.** **D.** 1946

**2.** **C.** Bedford Falls, New York

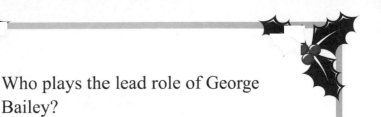

**3.** Who plays the lead role of George Bailey?

    **A.** James Stewart
    **B.** Gregory Peck
    **C.** Cary Grant
    **D.** Humphrey Bogart

**4.** How does George lose his hearing in one ear?

    **A.** He is hit in the head during a confrontation with bullies
    **B.** He rescued his younger brother from drowning in a frozen lake
    **C.** He ran into a stop sign while riding his bike as a child
    **D.** He was born without hearing in one ear

**5.** Why does Mr. Gower almost fill a prescription with poison?

    **A.** He is seeking vengeance on an enemy
    **B.** He is getting old and can't read labels very well
    **C.** He is experimenting with a new mixture of drugs
    **D.** He is upset over the death of his son

. . . . . . . . . . . . . . . . . . . . . . . . . . . . . . . . . . . . .

**3.** **A.** James Stewart

**4.** **B.** He rescued his younger brother from drowning in a frozen lake

**5.** **D.** He is upset over the death of his son

**6.** Why does George postpone his plans to attend college and travel the world on the night of Harry's high school graduation?

    **A.** He falls in love with Mary

    **B.** His mother dies

    **C.** His father dies

    **D.** He decides he likes Bedford Falls and does not want to leave

**7.** What is Clarence the angel promised if he can save George from killing himself?

    **A.** He will become a Superangel

    **B.** He will get his wings

    **C.** He will get his halo

    **D.** He can return to earth as a human

**8.** Where do George and Mary go on their honeymoon?

    **A.** Niagara Falls

    **B.** Hawaii

    **C.** They do not go anywhere

    **D.** Cape Cod

## ANSWERS

· · · · · · · · · · · · · · · · · · · · · · · · · · · · · · · · · · · · · · · ·

**6.** **C.** His father dies

**7.** **B.** He will get his wings

**8.** **C.** They do not go anywhere

**9.** What is the affordable housing project started by George called?

    **A.** Bailey Park

    **B.** Bailey Land

    **C.** Bailey Homes

    **D.** Bailey Condominiums

**10.** Why does George turn down Mr. Potter's offer of a $20,000 a year job and opportunities to travel the world?

    **A.** Mary is having a baby

    **B.** If George leaves, Mr. Potter will take over Bedford Falls

    **C.** It's not a big enough salary

    **D.** The world is in the middle of a war and George thinks it best not to do any traveling

**11.** How many children do George and Mary have?

    **A.** One

    **B.** Two

    **C.** Three

    **D.** Four

· · · · · · · · · · · · · · · · · · · · · · · · · · · · · · · · · · ·

**9.**   **A.**   Bailey Park

**10.**   **B.**   If George leaves, Mr. Potter will take over Bedford Falls

**11.**   **D.**   Four

**12.** Why can George not enlist in the military?

    **A.** He is too old
    **B.** Because of his bad ear
    **C.** He has too many kids to support
    **D.** He has flat feet

**13.** What award does Harry receive as a Navy fighter pilot?

    **A.** The Purple Heart
    **B.** The Bronze Star
    **C.** The Medal of Honor
    **D.** The Navy Cross

**14.** Why does George attempt suicide?

    **A.** He has been depressed since he was a young boy
    **B.** Because his family could collect life insurance on him
    **C.** A reason is never provided
    **D.** He misses his father

# ANSWERS

......................................................

**12.** **B.** Because of his bad ear

**13.** **C.** The Medal of Honor

**14.** **B.** Because his family could collect life insurance on him

**15.** When Clarence shows George what Bedford Falls would be like if he had never been born, which is NOT one of the consequences?

   **A.** Bailey Park is never built
   **B.** Mr. Gower goes to prison
   **C.** Mary is a spinster librarian
   **D.** The town is overrun by rats

**16.** How does George get enough money to save his business?

   **A.** His friends and neighbors donate it
   **B.** A wealthy relative dies and leaves him all her money
   **C.** He gets a high-paying job in New York City
   **D.** Mary sells her engagement ring

**17.** What book does George find a copy of at the end of the film?

   **A.** *Huckleberry Finn*
   **B.** *Of Mice and Men*
   **C.** *The Adventures of Tom Sawyer*
   **D.** *The Grapes of Wrath*

# ANSWERS

· · · · · · · · · · · · · · · · · · · · · · · · · · · · · · · · · · · · ·

**15.** **D.** The town is overrun by rats

**16.** **A.** His friends and neighbors donate it

**17.** **C.** *The Adventures of Tom Sawyer*

## 18. TRUE OR FALSE:

*It's a Wonderful Life* broke holiday movie sales records at the box office.

## 19. TRUE OR FALSE:

This is one of Frank Capra's personal favorite films.

## 20. TRUE OR FALSE:

Every time a bell rings, an angel learns to sing.

## 21. TRUE OR FALSE:

*It's a Wonderful Life* is based on a short story.

## 22. TRUE OR FALSE:

The film received five Academy Award nominations, but lost in every category.

## ANSWERS

· · · · · · · · · · · · · · · · · · · · · · · · · · · · · · · · · · · · ·

**18.**   **FALSE:**   It performed poorly at the box office, despite now being one of the most beloved movies of all time.

**19.**   **TRUE**

**20.**   **FALSE:**   Every time a bell rings, an angel gets its wings.

**21.**   **TRUE**

**22.**   **TRUE**

### 23. TRUE OR FALSE:

When Clarence shows George Bedford Falls in a universe where George was never born, the name of the town is Potter Park.

### 24. TRUE OR FALSE:

The role of Mary was the first starring role of Donna Reed.

### 25. TRUE OR FALSE:

Uncle Billy loses $10,000 of bank money, which results in criminal charges for George.

### 26. TRUE OR FALSE:

In the alternate universe of Bedford Falls without George, Harry is the only character who is still thriving.

### 27. TRUE OR FALSE:

Clarence ends up getting his promotion in the end.

## ANSWERS

........................................

**23.** **FALSE:** The town is called Pottersville.

**24.** **TRUE**

**25.** **FALSE:** Uncle Billy loses $8,000.

**26.** **FALSE:** Harry would have died had George not saved him from drowning.

**27.** **TRUE**

# Bad Santa

1. In what year did *Bad Santa* come out?
   - **A.** 2001
   - **B.** 2002
   - **C.** 2003
   - **D.** 2004

2. Who plays the role of Willie T. Soke?
   - **A.** Billy Bob Thornton
   - **B.** Brad Pitt
   - **C.** Ben Affleck
   - **D.** Johnny Depp

1. **C.** 2003

2. **A.** Billy Bob Thornton

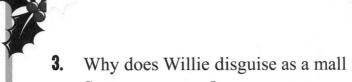

**3.** Why does Willie disguise as a mall Santa every year?

    **A.** It's his job
    **B.** To spread Christmas spirit
    **C.** To rob the mall
    **D.** He's homeless and likes to sleep in the mall in the winter

**4.** What is the name of the boy who actually thinks Willie is Santa?

    **A.** Harry Barry
    **B.** Miller Shiller
    **C.** Thurman Merman
    **D.** Johnny Salami

**5.** Who plays the role of Sue, the woman with a Santa fetish?

    **A.** Mandy Moore
    **B.** Amy Smart
    **C.** Anna Faris
    **D.** Lauren Graham

· · · · · · · · · · · · · · · · · · · · · · · · · · · · · · · · · ·

**3.**    **C.**    To rob the mall

**4.**    **C.**    Thurman Merman

**5.**    **D.**    Lauren Graham

**6.** Thurman says his father is away exploring mountains, but where is he really?

    **A.** He has a second family in Ohio
    **B.** He is a secret agent in the FBI and his location cannot be disclosed
    **C.** He died many years ago
    **D.** He is in jail for embezzlement

**7.** Where does Willie go to live when he sees his motel room being raided?

    **A.** The mall
    **B.** Thurman's house
    **C.** His mother's house
    **D.** The streets

**8.** What does Willie trick Thurman into letting him steal?

    **A.** A priceless family heirloom
    **B.** A BMW
    **C.** A one-of-a-kind painting
    **D.** A vacuum cleaner

# ANSWERS

**6.** **D.** He is in jail for embezzlement

**7.** **B.** Thurman's house

**8.** **B.** A BMW

**9.** How does Willie attempt to commit suicide?

    **A.** Overdosing on pills
    **B.** Shooting himself
    **C.** Inhaling vehicle exhaust fumes
    **D.** Walking into traffic

**10.** What does Willie get Thurman for Christmas?

    **A.** A blue stuffed koala
    **B.** A pink stuffed elephant
    **C.** A purple stuffed panda
    **D.** A yellow stuffed kangaroo

**11.** What does Marcus reveal to Willie toward the end of the film?

    **A.** He is having an affair with Willie's wife
    **B.** He is actually a spy
    **C.** He hired Thurman to act like an innocent child in order to trick Willie
    **D.** He plans to kill Willie

## ANSWERS

**9.**    **C.**    Inhaling vehicle exhaust fumes

**10.**    **B.**    A pink stuffed elephant

**11.**    **D.**    He plans to kill Willie

**12.** Why does Willie lead the police to Thurman's home?

   **A.** He knows they will not shoot him in front of a child
   **B.** He wants to give Thurman his present
   **C.** Thurman's house has bullet-proof walls
   **D.** He hopes to place all the blame on Thurman

**13.** Why are the police embarrassed after the shoot-out?

   **A.** They shot an unarmed Santa
   **B.** There was a real crime happening next door that they were too distracted to stop
   **C.** They missed their target
   **D.** They accidentally shot Thurman

**14.** What job does Willie get at the end of the film?

   **A.** Professional mall Santa
   **B.** Professional getaway driver
   **C.** Sensitivity counselor for the police
   **D.** Police paperwork filer

# ANSWERS

........................................................

**12.** **B.** He wants to give Thurman his present

**13.** **A.** They shot an unarmed Santa

**14.** **C.** Sensitivity counselor for the police

**15. TRUE OR FALSE:**

*Bad Santa* was John Ritter's last film appearance before his death.

**16. TRUE OR FALSE:**

Thurman stands up to his bullies at the end of the film.

**17. TRUE OR FALSE:**

Billy Bob Thornton won a Golden Globe Award for Best Actor for his role in the film.

**18. TRUE OR FALSE:**

A sequel to *Bad Santa* was released in 2016.

# ANSWERS

............................................

**15.** **TRUE**

**16.** **TRUE**

**17.** **FALSE:** Although he was nominated for the Golden Globe, Thornton lost out to Bill Murray.

**18.** **TRUE**

# The Polar Express

**1.** What year was The Polar Express released?

    **A.** 2001

    **B.** 2002

    **C.** 2003

    **D.** 2004

**2.** The film is based on a book of the same name by Chris Van Allsburg. What year did the book come out?

    **A.** 1984

    **B.** 1985

    **C.** 1986

    **D.** 1987

**3.** Where is Hero Boy from?

    **A.** Ann Arbor, Michigan

    **B.** Detroit, Michigan

    **C.** Grand Rapids, Michigan

    **D.** Harbor Springs, Michigan

## ANSWERS

· · · · · · · · · · · · · · · · · · · · · · · · · · · · · · · · · · · · · · ·

**1.** **D.** 2004

**2.** **B.** 1985

**3.** **C.** Grand Rapids, Michigan

**4.** What is the name of the impoverished boy whom the train picks up?

    **A.** Danny
    **B.** Billy
    **C.** Bobby
    **D.** Freddy

**5.** Who stows away a mug of hot chocolate to save for Billy?

    **A.** Hero Boy
    **B.** Hero Girl
    **C.** The Conductor
    **D.** Santa Claus

**6.** Who does Hero Boy meet on the roof of the train?

    **A.** A hobo
    **B.** Santa Claus
    **C.** A ghost
    **D.** God

**7.** What are the names of the engineers who replace the train's headlight?

    **A.** Smokey and Steamer
    **B.** Steamy and Smoker
    **C.** Foggy and Freighty
    **D.** Loco and Motive

# ANSWERS

..............................................

**4.** **B.** Billy

**5.** **B.** Hero Girl

**6.** **A.** A hobo

**7.** **A.** Smokey and Steamer

8. Who does Hero Boy encounter a puppet version of?

    **A.** Santa Claus

    **B.** Jack Frost

    **C.** Mother Nature

    **D.** Ebenezer Scrooge

9. What do the engineers use to repair the train's throttle?

    **A.** A safety pin

    **B.** A hairpin

    **C.** A clothespin

    **D.** A pushpin

10. How are the presents in the North Pole transported?

    **A.** By train

    **B.** By car

    **C.** By blimp

    **D.** By helicopter

11. Hero Boy receives a bell from Santa. What do his parents think is wrong with it?

    **A.** It's dirty

    **B.** It's broken

    **C.** It's ugly

    **D.** They think he stole it

# ANSWERS

............................................

**8.**    **D.**   Ebenezer Scrooge

**9.**    **B.**   A hairpin

**10.**   **C.**   By blimp

**11.**   **B.**   It's broken

## 12. TRUE OR FALSE:

Tom Hanks plays four different roles in the film.

## 13. TRUE OR FALSE:

When the boy first sees the train, he enthusiastically jumps on board right away.

## 14. TRUE OR FALSE:

Chris Van Allsburg, the author of the book *The Polar Express,* died before the movie was made.

## 15. TRUE OR FALSE:

At the time *The Polar Express* was made, its budget was record-breaking for an animated feature.

## 16. TRUE OR FALSE:

The roles of Smokey/Steamer were the last roles Michael Jeter played before his death.

# ANSWERS

**12.** **FALSE:** He plays six roles.

**13.** **FALSE:** He initially declines riding the train.

**14.** **FALSE:** Van Allsburg served as one of the executive producers on the film.

**15.** **TRUE**

**16.** **TRUE**

### 17. TRUE OR FALSE:

The conductor must disperse a herd of reindeer from the train tracks.

### 18. TRUE OR FALSE:

When Hero Boy meets the hobo on the roof, the hobo offers him hot chocolate.

### 19. TRUE OR FALSE:

Only those who truly believe in Santa can hear the bell ring.

### 20. TRUE OR FALSE:

*The Polar Express* received three Academy Awards.

### 21. TRUE OR FALSE:

The architecture of the animated buildings in the North Pole are based on real buildings in American railroading history.

## ANSWERS

**17.** **FALSE:** He must disperse a herd of caribou.

**18.** **FALSE:** The hobo offers Hero Boy coffee.

**19.** **TRUE**

**20.** **FALSE:** Although it was nominated for three Academy Awards, it did not win any of them.

**21.** **TRUE**